BODY LANGUAGE
IN
LOVE
AND
ROMANCE

(FINDING THE LOVE OF YOUR LIFE)

BY

JACQUELINE A. RANKIN, Ed. D.

ACKNOWLEDGEMENTS

Sonnet 116

"Let me not to the marriage of true minds
Admit impediments. Love is not love
Which alters when alteration finds,
Or bends with the remover to remove.
No! it is an ever-fixed mark
That looks on tempests, and is never shaken;
It is the star to every wandering bark,
Whose worth's unknown, although his height be taken.
Love's not Time's fool, though rosy lips and cheeks
Within his bending sickle's compass come;
Love alters not with his brief hours and weeks,
But bears it out even to the edge of doom.
If this be error and upon me proved,
I never writ, nor no man ever loved."

William Shakespeare

****

To my grandchildren, Borschels all –

Greg and Tina
Amanda
David
Alex
Sylvie

May your lives be filled with love!

-Jackie

Rankin File
7006 Elkton Drive
Springfield, Virginia, 22152
www.jrbodylanguage.com

ISBN 1-887711-01-5 –(4th printing, 2001)
Copyright Txu 797-963 (4/97)
(703) 866-0084
rankinj@potomacnet.com

TABLE OF CONTENTS

BODY LANGUAGE IN LOVE AND ROMANCE

(FINDING THE LOVE OF YOUR LIFE)

CHAPTER ONE - INTRODUCTION

Does the gold (not brass) ring at the end of the merry-go-round of life evade your grasp every time you grab for it? You are not alone in wishing for love... amour... an enduring emotional attachment in your life! Humans are sexy, sex-starved creatures constantly yearning to find a partner. Some famous people have had a great deal to say about love and romance:

"Sex is an emotion in motion." - Mae West.

"Marriage is the deep, deep peace of the double bed after the hurly-burly of the *chaise longue*." -Mrs. Patrick Campbell.

"Sex – the poor man's polo." - Clifford Odets.

"People who throw kisses are hopelessly lazy." - Bob Hope

"The one thing we can never get enough of is love. And the one thing we never give enough of is love." - Henry Miller.

"Though a man excels in everything, unless he has been a lover his life is lonely, and he may be likened to a jewelled cup which can contain no wine." - Yoshida Kenko.

"For one human being to love another: that is perhaps the most difficult of all our tasks, the ultimate, the last test and proof, the work for which all other work is but preparation." - Rainer Maria Rilke.

"Nobody has ever measured, even poets, how much a heart can hold." - Zelda Fizgerald.

Choosing the love of your life is the most important decision of your life and yet no one advises you academically how to make it, no classes seem to teach it, and there is no one to guide you regarding how to make that choice wisely. That is what this training manual is all about: how to choose your love partner through the oldest of all languages you speak, body language. I will endeavor to serve as your coach, teaching you how to assess others astutely. One wonders how I think I have the smarts to help you? I'm a divorcee, a body language expert who speaks to thousands of singles all over the country, and from my own experiences, education, academic research, bumps, bruises, and rubbing shoulders with others, I've arrived at the information contained in this little book. Learn from my bumps and bruises; use the knowledge to help you make the wisest decision of your life!

Body language is silent and speechless, yet it reveals different information than do words. Speech tells us what is the speaker consciously wants us to know; body language reveals what is the <u>unconscious</u> of the communicator. From body language, we can determine the communicator's basic personality, his role in various situations, the tenor of his thoughts (even the where, when, and sometimes the why), his role in interrelationships, even his value system —(what is really in his heart and head). I can tell if a subject is a truth teller just by his body language. When aiding attorneys in choosing juries, one looks for openness in the body language of the interviewee so that they will hear both sides of a legal argument. I teach salespeople to look for closure time by the use of body language and when to stall, waiting for the "aha!" moment. Health care staffs need to read the body language of the patient. Teachers need to decipher students' nonverbal systems. The list never ends of those who need to incorporate body language know-how in their lives.

If you do display negative, cold, closed body language, and results prove it, can you change your mannerisms and behaviors? *You bet your life you can.* As you decide some behavior is unsuccessful, you must then <u>consciously</u> decide to practice the correct behavior you seek. When we get to the section on "The Super You" we'll explore this further. Right now let's delve into Love and Romance, starting with ancient days.

It's been a long time since a fellow took a club to his maiden fair, dragged her by the hair back to his cave where thereupon they pursued love, romance, sex or whatever they had on their minds in that time of yore. Yet, any way you look at it, that's pretty much what happens today, the turn of the 21st century! Falling in love, the dull old experts say, is a mutual attraction acted upon by whatever appropriate actions are sanctioned by one's own peculiar time and place. Then the passionate sparks fly. It all sounds so simple, doesn't it?

Oh, if those dull old experts really knew!

2

Whatever your status that finds you alone:

...Divorced

...Widowed or bereaved

...Bereft of a loving relationship

...Unable to relate to others

...Separated

...Still striving to attract someone else--

Do not despair, this little training manual is here to help you. With it you can learn to read a stranger's body language as well as program yourself more effectively. Plan to be a winner at that critical initial encounter.

As you get into the next section of the book try to get a fix on yourself, the real you, not the pretty pulled-in tummy, chin up artificially pose – but rather the image we all see of you when you are least aware. Pull out old photos of yourself so that you can check your body language in those images and attempt to see yourself as the world sees you candidly. Check your reflection in mirrors. Be a super sleuth on the trail of the undeniable you. Make it an avid hunt.

Psychologically, you're an interesting subject. If you're feeling in the dumps, the image the world sees of you will be equally as down and unflattering. If you are feeling up, your self-image will match that image accordingly. The nonverbal message we send forth, whether we like it or not, accurately reflects our inner self. I remember after a long marriage and a sad breakup, I saw myself as fat, ugly, and dumb. Over and out. Several years later I checked photos of myself made at the time of the breakup and I could not believe reality. I weighed 110 pounds, so fat was out. With advanced degrees, dumb did not seem a fair adjective. Pride helped me throw ugly out. So I had allowed myself to be programmed negatively. Never again.

What about you? What negatives are you accepting into your life that do you no good? ..Be a detective and try to root out those poisonous negatives – they are toxic to your very well-being! We must learn to program ourselves positively. I felt a whole lot better after I studied those photos, believe me; (and that study was hard work). No one is ever going to program me negatively again. I won't allow it. I value myself too highly to let it happen.

This little books is about bringing creativity into your life and using it every minute of every day. Dan Wakefield says, "Creativity is the ability to transcend traditional ideas, rules, patterns, and relationships and to create meaningful new ones. In the larger sense, creativity makes us quintessentially human. As human beings, we have free will that enables us to create our own destiny and the capacity to depart from the status quo through acts of creative innovation."

If life seems unbearable right now, tell yourself you have nowhere to go but up. Are you sick and tired of seeing the world in pairs, in twos, as couples side by side? There was a time I hated to go to movies: In the darkened theatre, curled up in my lonely seat, I had to peer through couples snuggling closely and it was hard to see the movie screen what with all the loving couples blocking my vision. Or so I thought. Curiously enough, now I like movies and seem to see few couples. My vision is no longer blocked by depression and loneliness. Go through despondency, feel desperate for just a minute, grab a fresh breath and then take a firm hold. From here on out, we are going places, set goals, and more importantly, achieve those goals. We are going to explore such things as the real you, strangers, how to enter the world of real love and companionship, and how to find your dear one for life. Hold on to your hat – it's going to be an exciting ride. Here we go!

QUIZ: YOUR STARTUP QUESTIONS

(It's tell the **truth** time. You're the only one who will read your answers.)

1- Do you listen to negative tapes playing in your head too often, tapes that say such things as, "You dummy! How could you make such a stupid mistake?" or "You do not deserve to win, you loser."

2- Do you feel that you have no free will, that life somehow determines your life's pathway?

3- Do you live in the past or the future --more than in the present?

4- Do you constantly dwell on past pains?

5- Do you have the ability to create your own destiny, or do these words seem just plain silly?

6- Are you capable of creative problem-solving? If you <u>are</u> capable, do you have the guts to tackle whatever formidable task lies ahead?

7- This is a hard question and takes some cogitation to answer correctly. What are the old, established patterns of your life? Who taught you these patterns? Are you a captive of these old routine methods? Do you think that at this point you can design some new patterns to break out of those old established parameters? (Tea instead of coffee, vegetarian instead of meat for a change, a different clothing style, perhaps even a new script for your dialogues?)

8- Is someone influencing you, coaching you, criticizing you and, darn it, you are marching to THEIR drum beat? Yes, I know, <u>I</u>'m coaching. Guilty. By the end of the book, get rid of me, too. Become your own coach and march to your own drum beat!

9- Write a short paragraph or two about yourself. Try to describe yourself, your habits, your strengths, your weaknesses as others see you.

10- Okay, I know you are probably no artist, but draw some kind of a sketch of yourself. You'll be surprised what it reveals about the inner you.

Hints: Study these answers as objectively as possible. You may even want to paste them in a journal somewhere just to remember where you were psychologically on this day. Label it "My Starting Day."

CHAPTER TWO - WHY BODY LANGUAGE?

Are you asking why the need to apply body language to the search for the love of your life? Because it is where **REAL** communication takes place! It's the best of all tools for reading or deciphering the other person as well as clueing yourself into your own message system. If you can't read the other person or know how people are reading you nonverbally, sorry, Super You, you haven't a clue as to what's happening. As the movie says, you're clueless. Listen up, now, because the following data may be the most important information you have ever received in your whole life!

Body language is where meeting people, showing interest, and falling in love all take place. It's our oldest language and probably has been around since prehistoric times. Everyone in the world has body language, knows some of what it means, but generally doesn't take much time to decipher it. Nonverbal communication constitutes all the ways we transmit information without using words. As that little fetus in your mother's womb, you communicated with mama nonverbally, so you've always used silent language, you just weren't overtly aware of it.

Body language is a powerful tool that can change the direction of your life, once you've decided to incorporate it into your total communication system. Psychologists tell me that the work I do with clients is faster at changing the person than psychological counseling. Body language works outside in; psychology work inside out. Body language know-how can alter your very being. It can create a better feeling toward people and actually reconstruct your attitudes in general toward more harmonious conclusions. With major body language shifts, people's reactions can be shaped more favorably with outstanding results. People will respond differently to you and more importantly, you will feel better about yourself in general. I've seen people's faces change with this training so that they look younger, healthier, saner (yes, I mean that), and more lovable. Do you look as though you enjoy life or is your general image that of Oscar the Grouch? Body language revisions can mold you into a friendly spirit, both attractive and attracting to people. Betcha. I've worked with countless thousands of people and have seen miracles wrought – all through body language know-how and diligent application.

One word of caution. Body language cannot "alphabetize" movements and behaviors so that you can read a person like a book. Reason? Humans are too changeable and contexts vary. Nonverbal communication is much more complicated than so simple an interpretation. One must study the context of the situation, the people and their backgrounds, and even the agenda for the negotiation. So, please do not think this book can be a one-occasion dictionary that can solve everything instantaneously for you. I wish life could be that simple. Much hard work is needed in order to bring about the knowledge you desire.

Ethics play a large role in body language utilization. Do not plan to manipulate others with your knowledge of nonverbal communication.. People are not that easily fooled, and can you afford to make enemies? Plan to be honest in your intentions and endeavors and concomitant results should be satisfactory for you. If you decide to be a trickster, then don't complain when results turn out disastrously. As ye sow, so shall ye reap.

Let's take a minute and review a bit about nonverbal communication and nonverbal behavior. Body language is some 2500 years old, coming to us from the Greeks who felt their orators spoke more effectively when they employed vigorous body language, revealing the *ethos* of the speaker. Revived in the 1950s by Dr. Ray Birdwhistell, the study of nonverbal communication has taken its place respectably as a discipline worthy of study and utilization in every field of life. It's a known fact that 65-95% of all effective communication is nonverbal, with words going only as high as 35%. The impact of that data, when you give it consideration, is awesome. So, for purposes of this training manual, body language is where the real Language of Love lives and exerts power. You fall in love nonverbally, so why not study this language consciously for successful usage in your life? In order for you to remember the impact of body language, I've made up an acronym for it. P-U-S-H.

P stands for <u>Powerful,</u> for that is exactly what silent language is: more powerful than sound, stronger than verbal communication.

U stands for <u>Unconscious</u> because that, too, is what body language is. The minute you program your behavior consciously, it is cold, plastic, and totally bereft of sincerity. Authentic body language is totally unprogrammed, natural, sincere, and is truthful.

S stands for <u>Silent</u> and that is what body language is: no sound, just like an old silent movie.

H stands for <u>Honest</u> and it's important to remember that all the body cannot lie all the time, so seek the part of the body that is telling the truth. Body language will reveal the truth for you if you use your eyes rigorously, not your ears.

One more piece of advice when you are searching. *Look more than you listen.* Often, words will lead you astray, giving you incorrect facts or downright lies. Do not be misled. Learn to read the body language of the other person because in so doing, you are reading the correct (silent) message. All the body cannot lie all the time, remember, so start prowling for the honest signals emanating from your subject.

Thus, this little book is about how to read the body language of the other person as well as program your own nonverbal communication system correctly. If your goal is still to find your soul mate, Dear Super You, perhaps words to ring in your ears while you conduct your search are from the 1549, Anno Domini, *Book of Common Prayer*'s Marriage Ceremony:

*" To have and to hold from this day forward,
for better for worse,
for richer for poorer,
in sickness and in health,
to love and cherish,
till death do us part."*

BODY LANGUAGE QUIZ

1- Who has been your role model in body language throughout your life? (Hint: whom do you move like, think like, react like, even, perhaps look like a bit?)

2- What does open, warm, friendly body language mean to you? Can you describe some of the parts of the body that make up that message and how they function?

3- Describe cold body language.

4- Can you describe the body language of the happiest person you know?

5- Now, describe the body language of the saddest person whom you know.

6- Why is body language such a powerful tool?

7- What kind of body language do you want your lover to display? Can you keep this description in mind as you hunt for the love of your life and not get led astray?

8- Can you make a handy list to refer to when it comes to body language behaviors displayed by the other person, checking items such as gender display, gestures, body leans, facial expression, eye behavior, usage of space, and touch.? Refer to this list often in your hunt.

9- Define body language.

CHAPTER THREE - LOVE VERSUS ROMANCE

Have you ever wondered why those glamorous romance books sell by the bucketful? Because, Dear Reader, they are about fantasy, myth, legend -- something that does not even approximate our hum-drum reality. If you are out to find a fleeting romantic fling that will fade with the sunrise, this book is not for you. If, on the other hand, you want **THE REAL THING**, (long-lasting love) then continue reading. Throw away all those figments of your imagination, discard all those illusory pipe dreams, and decide not to be deluded any more. The popular media would have you believe that romance is what you are seeking, but when you fall prey to a momentary passionate fling, you're left right back where you started. Alone. Don't break your heart pursuing a self-aggrandizing romantic caprice -- it just separates you from valuable love..

Take a look at the differences between Romance and Love and try to determine where your mind and your life have been focused:

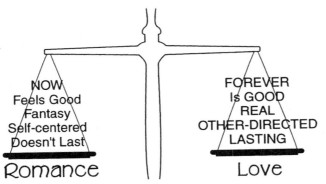

Keep in mind that authentic love has warts, wrinkles, some pain along with the good, ups with the downs, or as the marriage vows say, "In sickness and in health, for richer, for poorer." Never-Never Land focuses on the temporary satiation of bodily desires, a feeling of euphoria, and a whole lot of self gratification both physical and mental. What a waste. Remember, Dorothy finally tired of the glitter of Oz and fervently wanted to return to Kansas, hard work, hardscrabble, and a _real_ life with a _real_ family.

Are your standards for the love of your life unrealistic? For instance, do you discard someone because they are not pretty enough to fit your exacting desires: are they too short, not educated enough, don't have a job at the level you want them to be? Is their attire JCPenney when you want Saks Fifth Avenue? Do they drink beer when you know only champagne will please you? If your desires are too demanding, Mr. Or Ms. Snooty, this book is not for you. Keep on your search for the Perfect Person, and you'll probably still be looking into your 60s. Incidentally, while you're scrutinizing, take a good look at **yourself**. Are you fitting your own standards? Are your goals too high, too mythical, too unreal for this mundane world? I maintain the professional, productive, happy auto mechanic is a better lover than a miserable, sour CEO with piles of gold in the bank. Go look and reserve a glance for yourself. And do some thinking.

In fairy tales the Prince saves Cinderella and they (of course!) live happily ever after. In literature, Jane Eyre meets Mr. Rochester in dangerously mysterious circumstances that almost kill her, and he's immediately her hero. Mr. Darcy gives up his aloof proud prejudices and wins Elizabeth Bennet. Why can't we all live like this in our absurd real lives? Because (alas!) life is not a romanticized fairy tale. The frogs you've been kissing just do not turn into princes or princesses, in case you've checked lately. They just remain frogs, the twits, mucking up our lives miserably.

Andrew Weil, M.D., defines love another way: "To love is to experience connection in its highest, purest form, but oh, how we abuse the word *love*, how we confuse loving with other feelings that take us back into the world of separateness and fragmentation." I call most of those feelings "glandular," meaning that our sexual selves surpass reason and self-governance, and turn into actions that will lead to pain. The poets call "in love" a mood of passing insanity, and perhaps they are correct. "Glandular" can get us as high as if one were on drugs, and one must finally know that highs do turn into lows. Is that what you will settle for – something temporary?

Jane Austen, one writer of love stories who believed in love, not transient romance, used to quote the Church of England's wedding ceremony thusly: "...not for carnal pleasures nor to be entered into lightly." Not a bad thought for today, some 180 years after Jane's Regency England. Not to be entered into lightly. That means not a Kleenex society, throwing away the good things for some temporary thrill. Not for carnal pleasures, not for bodily gratification, not for passion nor for sensual pleasures. Hmmm. Food for thought for those who had thought that romance is the end-all and the be-all.

But isn't romance wonderful? You bet, as long as it lasts. Frances Vaughan thinks that falling in love is a spiritual awakening, showing us a profound sense of connection with another person, a kind of recognition, a sense of being joined. But once the honeymoon period is over, the differences between the personalities of the two lovers become apparent and then dissatisfaction sets in. Vaughan feels everyone has a shadow side, that no one is perfect. Happiness cannot come from another person. Real love sees our partner as a whole person, a separate individual with whom we <u>share</u> life's journey.

Another caution. Do not, <u>please</u>, project qualities you admire into the other person when such qualities do not exist, but are rather mere figments of your overactive imagination. I've done it and come a cropper because when your consciousness comes alive after a romantic interlude, you cannot believe what your storybook romance has become in daylight's harsh reality. You'll end up moaning in your pillow, "How could I have done that!" futilely. Accessing reality is a painful process and one learns that molding people into marionettes is an exercise in futility.

I believe in the Law of Attraction, the principle of like attracting like, so prepare yourself mentally to be positive, to behave optimistically, and above all, to put forth happy body language that conveys your positive outlook on life. Gloom attracts Sad Sues or Pitiful Pauls and if you don't believe it, put the Law to the test at a singles' social event. If you look mean, temperish, impatient, or like a loser, giving forth that message nonverbally, plan to attract someone almost like yourself. (Yep, can't resist it: you attracted and you earned it!) Then at the next event, put on a happy face, demeanor and body language and see whom you attract. Live a positive image and dare to reap the golden results!

As the song lyricist cautions us:

"You've gotta win a little,
You've gotta lose a little...
That's the story of - -
That's the story of
LOVE !"

CHAPTER FOUR - THE SUPER YOU

"If you bring forth what is within you, what you bring forth will save you. If you do not bring forth what is within you, what you do not bring forth will destroy you."
- Jesus the Christ, *Gospel of Thomas*, The Gnostic Nag Hammadi Library - Coptic Museum, Cairo, Egypt.

If you're going to capture the gold ring on the merry-go-round of life, you'll have to see yourself as a wonderful piece of merchandise which you will be compelled to design yourself. I urge you to package, color, refine, and market it. See yourself as a unique marvel, a one-of-a-kind miracle who comes along just once, even into infinity. Realize there will be stiff competition out there (especially so for women), and that's tolerable because your product is superb. We'll call that new you **THE SUPER YOU** .

Think about what topics becloud you and start cleaning them out of your consciousness. Let go of the past also. If you are caring too much about tragedies that occurred yesterday, are you aware that you are wearing those old melodramas on your face, in your posture, and even in sad eyes? Dump that sadness because it attracts no one. Turn off the tapes in your head that lure you into telling another sad tale about yourself. I know because I've been there and done that. After a whole series of major tragedies in my life, I found myself telling my story one time too many: A dear friend inadvertently (I hope) yawned in my face. And in my head I thought: "Jackie, have you become dull and boring on top of everything else? Patty is yawning out of boredom." Thud. Boring is a capital offense in my world. I changed those mental tapes and decided to clear my head of me-centered tragedies. We've all had our share of tough times, but as Dr. Robert Schuller loves to say, "Tough times don't last: tough people do."

In becoming a more positive you, construct a game plan. Are you living too much in dreams instead of setting practical goals? Do you have even a single strategy for success in your kit bag? Are you practicing winning strategies? Are you designing more successful body language moves? How are your alternative strategies? When one plan fails, are you constructing another to take its place? Are your practices evolving into solid habits? Charlie Brown says: "Life is like an ice cream cone, you have to lick it one day at a time."

It's time for an attitude check. Are you answering my questions with, "I don't need that." Or are you thinking, "It sounds like too much hard work. I don't want to put that much effort into such a change!" Or are you silently mouthing, "Who knows? Maybe I won't like myself if I change too much." All your mutterings are silent prohibitive chatter trying to hold you back. Do your life results prove you do need to change? Assess your present status and see if this is where you want to be. Let us try at this point to see how you perceive yourself: your mannerisms, behaviors, hang-ups, strengths, and weaknesses:

SELF-IMAGE QUIZ

Just for a minute, try to get a handle on your Self-Image. See how you answer the following questions:

1- When you enter a room, do people look at you in a friendly manner?
2- Is your posture erect, or are you slumped hollow-chestedly most of the time?
3- Do you make eye contact easily with strangers or do you avoid strangers like the plague?
4- Do you often make excuses for yourself?
5- Worse yet, do you blame others for your mistakes? Do you believe your goofy excuses?
6- Do you have quite a few good friends?
7- Are you happy with your job?
8- Do people appreciate you?
9- Do you consider your life good?
10- Can you accept a compliment gracefully?
11- Do you avoid social events, preferring to stay home alone?
12- Do you laugh twice as much as you cry?

You get the point. In surveying your life and your attitudes that shape your life, you can readily ascertain as to whether you are a Winner or a Loser. Losers whine. Losers make excuses for their own mistakes. Losers often lie to themselves, and poor souls, sometimes even enticed by comfortable lies, believe those pathetic distortions. Losers do not attract people. Losers go around unhappy with life and its myriad problems. Sorry to say it, but losers are a mess. Now on the other hand, winners are interesting people to study. They can come from shabby, tragic backgrounds and determine to prevail, almost like a bright red geranium valiantly growing from a dunghill. Winners are exciting people to be around. They are dynamic and seem to draw energy from the universe. Winners smile at strangers, touch easily, and give more than they receive. Winners are creative problem-solvers. Winners strive constantly to be Winners. Winners, in brief, are anything but a mess. Let's take a look at how losers become losers.

NEGATIVE MIND SETS

Some negative mind-sets Newburger and Lee advise us to be wary of are:

1- DEPRESSIONS

This is impounded or hidden anger stuck down in the nether regions of the psyche. ("I'm no good, you hear? Maybe I should just end it all.! I can't take this another minute!") Sometimes a sense of hopelessness pervades the depths of the depressed person. Sources for the emotion are many: the tragic death of a loved one can bring a heavy onslaught of paralyzing depression, but normally after a period of mourning, we begin to emerge slowly out of the gloomy tunnel. Other stimuli can be loss of a job, divorce, even bankruptcy. Some of us become angry instead of lethargic when we do not fulfill our dreams or potentials, and this type of depression does not propel us forward into productivity. Hostile body language, remember, frightens the liver out of our viewers. Whatever type of depression you undergo, it must be rooted out of your life.

People in our lives can threaten us in mysterious ways and we can perhaps have trouble moving beyond them and the resultant gloom that descends upon us. Sometimes, whatever the cause, we nurse that hidden anger and life gets blacker and blacker. ("Life is just no good. People are no blasted good! I'm no good.")

For those of who have been divorced, bereft, dumped, or find ourselves alone for some other reason, a long period of intense loneliness can bring on depression. I went through a period of feeling very much alone and deeply depressed, and I know such a state is serious. Be with other people and tell them your feelings plainly. Professional help may be needed, but realize you must not stay depressed and lonely for too long a time. Please reach out for aid if you need it. Do not waste time trying to patch up yourself if depression is long-lasting or all-engulfing.

Depression robs us of positive energy and we need to seek help in order to escape its lethal confines that produce a negative self-image. Stop it. Stomp on those poisonous thoughts every time they yell at you. Start sticking up for yourself and feel just how energizing an experience it is to place yourself as #1 for a change. You deserve the best! Hey, <u>you are the best</u>!

2- ANXIETY

Here you experience a sense of deep-rooted insecurity as though you are unbalanced or unstable. You feel strangely off kilter. This emotion is based on fear that you won't attain your potential, that you are letting others down, and that you are not bringing out your talents and skills to their fullest. Three instances where anxiety, almost panic, can grab hold of us, are just before making a speech, playing a part on stage, or meeting a stranger. There are solutions for such stresses. I try to teach students to **USE** anxiety, to allow its energy to propel you just as a race horse uses his pent-up feelings at the starting post. When used positively, anxiety can make you a winner with that extra boost of energy it bestows upon you. Anxiety has a certain sense of thrill about it, so experience that boost also. If used negatively, anxiety can induce you to doubt your worth and shape you into becoming a loser at whatever endeavor you are tackling. With practice, you can turn anxiety into a friend.

3- NON-ASSERTION

I call this the red carpet syndrome. This is the bad habit that allows others to walk all over you because you will not stand up for yourself. Tsk. Tsk. You want people to like you so much that you give your whole ball game away heedlessly. Let's face it: you are really saying, "Go ahead! Use me!" You do not know the word "no" even when it can protect you. Yessing is doing you in. Non-assertion buys peace at any price -- I don't even call that "an honorable peace."

If you're playing any of these non-defensive games, you do not have a winning personality yet, and until you are ready, you cannot attract a good, kind, loving winner. A house must have a firm foundation in order to withstand the storms it will endure. So must your life.

What are some of the dreadful qualities you display openly if you want to attract a loser? Nonverbally, you emit the message, "Okay, so I'm a red carpet. Please walk all over me." You react, not act. You seldom call the shots. You do not experience how energizing it feels to place yourself **#1**. Non-assertives often see themselves as the bottom of a priority list. You _feel_ like a failure, you _move_ like a loser, and _you even look like a failure_. People read that nonverbal message loud and clear. As a result, your relationships usually end in sorrow and "Guess what," you say to yourself, "I lost again." Remember, no one can force you to be a doormat: you yourself give permission for such a hostile masochistic act, so stop permitting yourself to be used. Learn the beautiful word "No." Only Ado Annie in "Oklahoma" could sing "I'm jist a gal who cain't say no!"... and smile about it.

4- SELF-SACRIFICE

"Oh, what I've done for you, you'll never know." Sound familiar? How about: "You owe me big time, buddy, and you'd better pay up." The Suffering Saintly Self-Sacrificer is a sorry pain-in-the-neck. Suffering succotash. This person sets up everybody as potential victims and sometimes gets away with it until he meets somebody who is a stout brick wall who won't play the game by his cockeyed rules. It's your choice. If you choose to be his victim, do not whine about it. Isn't life strange? You can aid others silently or be a loudmouth manipulator who blatantly wants everyone's adoration. Give silently and just maybe you will receive. Give loudly expecting adulation and you'll find yourself playing your marble game alone.

One of the saddest stories I've known was when as a high school teacher ,I listened to a huge six foot bruiser of a football hero sit in my classroom after school. He cried heartrendingly over his guilt at hurting his mother when he was born. (You read that right.) I tried to persuade him that a little baby does not determine the status of its birth. That his guilt was old ma's manipulation. "But, " he sobbed, "I ruined her life." It took some work but I turned him around. Mom will have to tell someone else her self-sacrificing story -- and find a victim. Joey is now free of guilt.

5- MISPLACED ANGER

You spilled a breakfast cup of coffee at home and then later angrily yelled at your secretary at the office for no reason at all. You just misplaced your anger, hitting the wrong target and nice people don't act that way. Another example: the car in front of you on the freeway cut you off so you then drive like a jerk, yelling and honking at all other drivers who dare to get near. You claim that such illogical anger makes you feel better. Listen up, Dude: you're expressing anger incorrectly and it earns you no friends. Such displays may make you feel better temporarily, blowing off steam on an innocent victim, but does that make such a display right? Does it make you a winner, gaining you friends, votes, money, or love? Weigh the consequences and if your anger continues to spout goofily, then suffer the smoldering hostility that will erupt all over you at a later date. Your displaced anger gets you nothing but enemies. Betcha.

I suggest people write the complaint, wad up the note, and keep throwing it around the room. Or, better yet, pile up some pillows in the corner and kick the stuffing out of them. Pillows are easier to replace than people. Pillows can't feel hurt the way people can.

6- ALIENATION

"I don't wanna play with you. You can't come to my house. My dolly is mine and you can't have her. You can't holler down my rain barrel nor slide down my cellar door. Nyaah, nyaah." Kids talk like this when they are pushing others away, but hopefully you are more mature than that. The alienated person is the ultimate loser because he has programmed a toxic game he can't possibly win, and it turns on him every time, just like a nasty old boomerang. Go ahead, sit alone and sulk. Make ugly faces at the world. Whine. Cry. But look around: is anybody even coming close to cold, closed, alienated, hostile you?

Well, then, what are some of the personality attributes that attract others **to** us? What characteristics attract you? Take a look at this "Good Stuff" list and see if you embody the list (or at least some of it) every day.

Look closely at some the persuasive characteristics that do not come easily to you. Make a list of them, pin it on your pillow, or tape it on the bathroom mirror. Drench yourself in some of the qualities you need to a greater degree in your life. Do not allow yourself to program your body language negatively any longer. Alienation just will not bring you love.

Think of ways to bring "Good Stuff" into your own personality. Love comes with those great qualities.

```
   +++         good stuff         +++

            CHEERFULNESS
              OPTIMISM
            FEARLESSNESS
           SELF-ASSERTION
      GIVING ( silently, please )
              OUTGOING
       CAREFULLY DIRECTED ANGER
            FRIENDLINESS
             EASY SMILER
              KINDNESS
              EMPATHY
```

"Ah," you say, "those sound like Girl Scout rules. What's so darned good about them?"

Do you go around saying things in your head directed to yourself only such as "Fool...dummy...loser?" Winners do not put themselves down. Winners constantly strive to rid themselves of self-defeating attitudes, replacing them with self-building thoughts. I recommend incorporating daily affirmations. Stand in front of the mirror and say to yourself seriously: "You are a winner! I like you! You are loving and lovable and you attract positive people into your life." (Do not be afraid of what others think about this exercise. That's their problem!) Whatever the negative emotion or thought is that is haunting you, confront it directly and stomp it out. What does all of this have to do with your body language? As you think, so will your image reflect those thoughts and attitudes to the public. The more optimistic you feel about yourself and the world, the friendlier your nonverbal message. Obviously, we are attracted to genuinely friendly people more than we are to pickle puss/cross patches.

Sadly, not everyone's feedback is filled with compliments. Occasionally someone in our lives gives us feedback that is critical, probably, so they hope, meant for our good. Do you pay such accurate criticism serious heed, as much as when you listen to the flowery compliments, or do you miss the truth? Have cohorts tried to let you know you are not behaving like a winner? If so, get to work. Pay attention. With such feedback, they were trying valiantly to help you. That fearless truth-teller is your friend.

Do not wait for the prince on the white charger or the golden haired princess in the tower. They are not hanging around to save you, Sweetie. **We do not derive our identity through another.** Got it? We have to walk the walk alone in order to come out a winner. That means tolerating our own company (and enjoying it, incidentally). That means enduring some grief silently, bravely, and alone. You are not a winner if you cannot tolerate your own presence. Try to get acquainted with yourself in pleasant circumstances. If you're in a dreary, boring lifestyle, get creative and plan some productive joy-filled occasions for yourself, by yourself. Find beautiful spots and photograph them. Talk to strangers about themselves and you'll meet a ton of people out there who are incredibly interesting. Learn a new skill: how about dancing? Work out that body physically so wonderful endorphins can fill your system with exhilaration. Forget yourself and help others. (Become a volunteer in a hospice and find out what real suffering is like.) Think about ways of improving yourself and your world positively. Until you have cleaned up your own act, you are not ready for a love relationship.

My greatest fear after my divorce was, crazy as it seems, to have breakfast alone. You see, I'd gone straight from college into marriage, and I'd never lived alone. So came the first morning in my condo and I fixed a palatable breakfast on my very best china, set up a Bible lesson beside my place mat, played a soft sonata in the background, and had a study/eat session. When I glanced at the clock and realized I'd spent the hour alone contentedly, a miracle had taken place in my consciousness. I could live alone and like it!

I'm a believer in the Principle of the Vacuum. (No, silly, not the cleaner type, the empty space kind.) Once one has carved out past debris from one's heart and soul, there is **then** room for something good to come fill that space. It works, believe me, it works in wondrous ways. Prepare that space for the love of your life; plan for that dear person to stay in your heart forever.

It's important as you build a Super You that you analyze how you come across to the stranger. Do you have your act together? Do you have an attractive look about yourself? Are you kempt? Is your wardrobe clean, colorful, and appropriate? Do you choose colors for yourself that are warm and appealing? Donna Karan can wear black seven days a week and get away with it, but who would want to look so bleak! Seriously do you wear your clothes or do your clothes wear you? Is your gender displayed tastefully? (We'll go into that in detail later.) Do you move in a graceful fashion? Is your smile wide and happy? Are your teeth clean? Is your breath fresh? Do you look well-groomed, pulled together artistically? Do you smell appealingly? Nosy questions, I'll concede, but ones you need to consider privately.

Happy thoughts in your head and warm feelings in your heart, believe it or not, make you more desirable to know. I very much believe implicitly that your own unprogrammed unconscious

18

body language conveys your inner attitudes, so a thin-lipped smile (or none), tightly clenched fists, tough or choppy gestures, an unappealing body odor, rude behavior, lack of respect for another person's personal space, a brazenly garish gender display all bespeak a person most polite society avoids. An optimistic attitude accompanied by positive words and kind behavior go a long way toward making friends, so make sure your first impression is warm and kind. Beware: most attachments are formed in the first impression, and I write about this in my book, *Body Language: First Impressions*. A stranger sizes up a stranger in less than a minute and that evaluation is a lasting one. That book goes into the fourteen variables by which one is adjudged: color, gender, size and shape, skull conformation, facial expressions, eyes, mouth, gestures, posture, critical leakages, territoriality, attire, that bugaboo smell, and even etiquette.

In addition, your computer brain is so fast in making assessments that you arrive at a final answer in a matter of seconds. All of these variables have a critical effect on your total image as you are perceived by someone else.

I've said it before: do not despair. It won't take much money to update your appearance. Mere money can't buy you new body language – only hard work will. But more importantly, changing your habits will take a lot of practice, self-control and hard effort. The changes won't take place overnight, but starting the changeovers can begin right now. It is all a matter of determination, motivation, and goal-setting. I make it sound easy, I know, but once you begin the habit of cleaning out negative thoughts, movements, and expressions, plan for phenomenal results.

I often work with clients who are metaphysically rudderless and <u>their body language tells us of the lack of balance</u>. I myself find that seeking the aid of our Higher Power can strengthen all aspects of our lives, but you must choose your own diagnosis and panacea. Prayer, meditation, yoga, walking in the woods, attending church or synagogue are some ways to reach Divine Mind. And peace and balance. When all human methods fail, higher meditation helps, I believe. You may be single, but with God you are never alone. And best of all, one with God is a majority!

Expect this section of the manual to take days, weeks, even months before you have yourself packaged correctly. Take it slowly and carefully. Check with someone whom you can trust to survey your progress and coach you honestly about what still needs improvement. Check photos, videotapes, mirror images and even window reflections for your own study. Whatever be brutally honest with yourself. Truth succeeds as self-deception never will.

   * <u>Practice smiling widely and openly</u>. I preach smile exercises to clients because Great Stone Faces look like losers. One client told me his mouth hurt when he first practiced smiling because his tight-lipped mouth was not accustomed to such strange mouth activity. "Good," I said, "Hurt. But keep smiling."

- Practice a friendly greeting and handshake. No standing in corners all forlorn. And, gals, this means you, too. Stick out your hand and shake the fellow's hand once or twice firmly. A smile and a touch are magic. Use my good old 1-2-3-4 Rule:

• THE GOOD OLD 1-2-3 4 GREETING RULE

1- STAND

2- MOVE TOWARD THE OTHER PERSON AND MAKE FIRM EYE CONTACT.

3- SMILE

4- STICK OUT YOUR HAND FOR A FIRM, FRIENDLY HANDSHAKE, MAINTAINING THAT PLEASANT FACIAL EXPRESSION AND EYE CONTACT.

- Practice direct eye contact with everyone you meet. No more furtive eyes. Don't stare too long (Mom told you not to), but do give a firm glance at one of his eyes. This is serious, I'm not kidding, look at only one of his eyes, not both. Both-staring results in crossed eyes which defeats the purpose of the whole exercise. Good calm, direct eyes: those are winners.

- Practice not giving in to shyness. Every time you overcome a shyness attack, reward yourself with something you've always wanted. The Kohinoor diamond, a Ferrari, or whatever.

- Practice making gentle, slow-moving gestures. No more harsh, threatening movements of the hands, please.

- Practice looking at strangers at social events, not boldly, but in an easy roaming manner surveying the room as though you are totally comfortable. Don't waste time staring at your shoes or the wall. For shy people, it's difficult dealing with folks, but you must deal with people visually. Practice good, strong, trusting eye contact, please.

- Practice displaying a brand new heart, not that old broken one any longer. Make your smiles turn up at the corners, don't tip your head to either side, sit or stand up straight, do not slump your shoulders, and take deep breaths in order to keep your voice firm and not quivery.

- Practice palm-up, not palm-down gestures with your hands. (More in a later section of the book.)

- Practice honest behavior that tells the truth when you have made an error in judgment. Do not be afraid to say you made a mistake. Hey, we're all human and we appreciate your forthrightness. Lying, cheating and stealing get you nowhere.

Susan Jeffers, Ph.D., author of *Feel the Fear and Do It Anyway* recommends switching "pain words" to "power words." "It's important," she says, "to monitor your words, using phrases that empower rather than weaken you." Check the following list and see what positive words swaps you can make in order to make your act more powerful.

Instead Of....	**Say**
I can't	I won't
I should	I could
It's a problem	It's an opportunity
Life's a struggle	Life's an adventure
I hope	I know
If only	Next time
What will I do?	I know I can handle it

Beyond mere words, think of strategies. <u>You can't market the new you if the right people don't get a chance even to see you.</u> Remember, we can't fall in love with someone across a crowded room if we don't set a foot into <u>that crowded room.</u> Do not overlook those who are bereft of a mate, who perhaps are separated, divorced, or single by choice or by fate. How do you know their status? Ask questions! Get acquainted a bit so you can ascertain their availability. It's that simple, and if you require confirmation, do a little detective work. One gal I know became suspicious of the doctor she was dating, and unexpectedly went to the office address printed on his business card. Lo and behold, when she asked for Dr. X, the reply was: "There's no Doctor X here. Joe X works here, and he's the office gofer." Hmmm. Her detective work saved her from a broken heart and who knows what else.

Where, you ask, do you meet people? I've made quite a study of this as I researched for this book, and my considered reply is just about anywhere decent. For real. No joke. The grocery store. Restaurants. The pet shop. The local animal shelter. Concerts. Stop signs. The Metro. Airplane flights. Sharing a cab. Amtrak. Square dancing. Wine tasting. Tour groups. Book clubs. Car pools. Softball games. Mensa groups. The Sierra Club. Habitat for Humanity work parties. Coffee bars. Dog shows. Country line dancing spots. Church. Classes of all kinds. Parking lots. Plays. Singles affairs sponsored by churches or synagogues. Political party work meetings or rallies. Sports clubs or sports events. Museums. Poetry readings. Karate classes. Skating rinks. Cooking schools. Racquetball clubs. Art classes or just you sketching in a park. Walking your dog. Window shopping. Food courts at the local mall. Showing off your cat somewhere. Photography classes or a solitary shoot you're on just snapping pictures outdoors. Garden shops or hardware stores especially when you're befuddled as to just what tool to choose.

It's important that you keep your mind alert to your task. It's easy to get off task and forget about looking for the love of your life. How many times were you dressed grungily and missed the love of your life? How often were you in a bad mood and didn't come across invitingly at all? How often we sail right by the person who could change our lives forever just because we were not thinking.

Ask friends about eligible single folk they can recommend. Try it: many a blind date has turned out happily. I do not recommend computer dating unless you meet the stranger personally accompanied by a trustworthy friend. Blind ads can sometimes end unhappily, and beware of Internet dating. Too many horror stories are printed in the media these days of innocent victims who were neither cautious nor careful. Better to be safe than sorry.

When you have accomplished all you can think of to polish **THE SUPER YOU**, you're just about ready for the next chapter. Remember those photos and videotapes I asked you to study? Pull them out again and try to figure what parts of your body language system need remedying in order for you to be superb.

Points to keep in mind as you build the Super You are:

Whatever the fear, feel that fear.

Courage grows the moment you face that fear.

Your fear can teach you lessons as you face it.

Courage is already inside you.

Listen to fear's message, then feel free to disagree.

Clarity increases with ongoing practice.

Fears that are ignored, denied, criticized, condemned, repressed, or minimized will grow.

Sometimes, caught unawares, you will forget what you know.

Regression is natural; the seed of courage is still within you – choose to cultivate it.

Success comes from practice, so go back to the first step again and again.

- Sarah Quigley
Finding Courage, 1996

CHAPTER FIVE - COURTSHIP

UNIVERSAL COURTING CUES

All humans smile. All humans cry. Some facial expressions are universal and the study of face and body behavior commenced with the great Charles Darwin well over a century ago. He really started us on the path of deciphering body clues. Modern researchers such as Morris, Marsh, and Molcho have led the way in looking at the human body, studying it and all its movements, and arriving at solutions to nonverbal riddles. And no one has contributed more fact-finding than my hero, Paul Ekman, in finding what the face says and what it hides.

The smile, the sequential flirt, the coy look, the head toss, the chest thrust, and the gaze have been around probably from time immemorial and constitute universal courting signals calculated to attract a mate. Incidentally, I think when cave man found that clubbing the girl of his dreams with a tree branch wasn't as much fun as idyllic fondling, he began to court the dear girl. Tree limb blows didn't equal finger dawdling. Thus began primitive courtship. I am sure that the love they found was more gratifying than the earlier episodes of mayhem, if you get my meaning. I do believe that he learned that courting resulted in better mating, and thus began our own rules of courtship. Romantic courtship can be magically joyous, so plan to live the Courtship Stage of your life to its fullest. I wish I could bottle up its ambiance for you to re-live the rest of your life, that's how delightful the act of courting is. Ask someone in the September era of their life about their courting days and watch the sparkle come to their eyes, fresh tone to the cheeks, and note their excited breathing as they describe the love-search days of their youth.

Helen Fisher has separated courting cues into five stages to which I've added some embellishments.

COURTING CUES

STAGE ONE- ATTENTION-GETTING

There are many ways to draw attention to oneself: seating postures, body leans, bold walks, or flamboyant facial expressions. All these movements say Look at me! just as do bold colors or brassy tones. One can pitch the walk, stretch the arms (or legs), bat the eyes, roll the shoulders, peek over a shoulder, and shift from one foot to the other in a fascinatingly swaying motion almost hypnotic in its allure. For instance, when one wants to draw the notice of someone else, instead of just a solitary arm movement, the whole body moves. Hearty laughter that incorporates the total body (and is loud enough to attract a crowd) draws attention, no doubt about it. That was the design when it was on the drawing board! In brief, every body movement is orchestrated resolutely and boldly. Is such behavior totally conscious? Probably not, for a lot of courting cues are totally unconscious, they just spring naturally from a fountain of emotions and thoughts. Take a glance at some of the signals:

A- The Swagger- The parading gait displayed here is a defiant or insolent strut. The swaggerer watches the other person out of the corner of his eye to be sure his audience is aware of his cockwalk. He (or she) will pat the hair, adjust the clothes, tug the chin, throw back the shoulders, self-clasp or use a self-grooming movement, all accompanied by a defiant bluster of a walk. The Swagger does draw attention extremely well and gets an A+ for effort.

B- Men and Props- Some men adorn themselves with expensive jewelry, clothing, *accoutrements,* if you will, that bespeak success. A silly pudding such as Britain's Prince Charles often adjusts his cufflinks endlessly, in case you've missed the point that he has riches and that he's even there. (He needs to read this book.) I used to become nauseous in California looking at grey masculine chest hairs slyly peeking through gold chains and medallions, with the collar gaping wide open clear down to the navel. The pathetic displayer thought he looked young and sexy. Maybe it was male menopause, who knows, but he felt he needed youthful props in order to fool the girls. Score: No Love.

C- Male Moves- Often resembling the female, but in a more brusque fashion, male courting moves are distinctive from those of the female. As dear old Mae West advised: It is better to be looked over than to be overlooked. Lots of lusty males refuse to be overlooked as they roam singles' hangouts. Smiles, soulful gazes, bold body shifts, swaying, preening, stretching, and moving into another's territory –all so that one can get a good look at the our lusty male subject-- All signal a male animal who is on the hunt. These male moves sometimes receive sizing-up looks in return from milady. (She's shopping, too, and heaven knows she was born to shop.) If he's really on the prowl, such as our rock stars on stage, his Taboo Zone (the area where the genitalia are contained) is brazenly displayed, just to let her know he is **MAN!**

D- Female Courting Walk - Think of Scarlett swishing her many beruffled hooped skirts, recall Clara Bow showing her rouged knees, think of Marilyn Monroe swinging those (ahem) little hips or imagine Cleopatra swaying (pre-asp) toward Antony. Women arch their backs gracefully, thrust out their bosoms tauntingly, sway their hips from side to side and strut their stuff just like a dancer in an old fashioned cakewalk. They move to a tantalizing inner beat no one else can hear but certainly can see! **WOMAN** is on the prowl, too, in her unique way.

Catherine de Medici, in the 1500s invented high-heeled, pain-filled shoes, that have given us gals an enticingly over-exaggerated walk, a clomping noise no male can mistake, and a beautifully sexy extended leg. Vanity, thy name is five inch heels. Accompany this high-heeled gait with puckered lips as though bee-stung, batting eyes with painted eyelashes, arched eyebrows, upturned palms, pigeon toes, and rocking bodies, accompanied by dancing hands that preen oneself about the bosom, swaying skirts, gleaming teeth, sensual perfumes, glowing skin – whew! **THE WOMAN** is plainly signaling approachability and perhaps even availability!

E- <u>Female Props</u> - Women cannot get off easily either, now that I've slammed the males who try to look inappropriately young. Nothing is sadder than an overaged gal who tries to look adolescent. The media is no help with its display of young fashions, faces, and bodies. But best take a good look at yourself, Lady, and try to have your image at least a decade in proximity to your chronological age. And if today's fashions are unflattering, wear something a little out of date but flattering. (Do you wear the clothes or do the clothes wear you?) That fashion will be in style soon anyway, if you watch what the sales games designers play.

Monitor yourself on the usage of cosmetics also. Too much is too much. Plaster troweled on too thickly looks exactly what it is. But (alas) too little is too little. You've got to be Baby Bear on this one: just right is just right, so it may take some expert advice to tell you about your face and its cosmetic needs. Keep Bette Davis' Baby Jane face in mind and do try to be a little less blatant.

STAGE TWO RECOGNITION

A- <u>Talk or Conversation</u>- After the primary body language first impressions, come the words. *Verbal is secondary to nonverbal.* If Stage Two does not succeed, then, all negotiations cease and our participants trot off to meet someone else. Words and the voice play a requisite role in courtship. The soft, purring voice (grooming talk) is idle in pace and content, often consisting of meaningless conversation, but it <u>is</u> going somewhere. The voices become higher, softer, more sing-songy, almost like a pigeon's cooing, rather like the very tones we use to express affection with children or pets. Check yourself out: you will be shocked how your voice changes when you are in a courtship mode.

B- <u>Remind Yourself</u> it is not so much WHAT you say as HOW you say it. This is critical. Talking can be very dangerous at this stage, so keep your remarks low-key.

STAGE THREE - GROOMING TALK

I know. I know. Talk is not body language, but I want to cover all possible corners for you. The title "Grooming Talk" comes to us from the great anthropologist, Desmond Morris, who has given us many books about animal and human behavior, incorporating facts about body language in new, fascinating ways. He has filmed courting couples all over the world and his research adds valuable information to anthropologists everywhere.

Morris says that potential love affairs often go astray soon after conversation starts. If you can weather this step, and each person begins to listen actively to the other, you move on to Stage Four. Listen to your voice. Fran Drescher with her nasalic Bronx accent AND braying laugh had better move back to Stage One despite her great body. I'm serious, if you need a voice coach, get one, please. A beautiful voice is your goal in Stage Three.

STAGE FOUR - TOUCHING

Now let's get back to body language again. Touching begins with sly little "inattention cues": leaning forward, resting one's arm toward the other's arm on a table, slyly moving one's foot closer, or seductively stroking one's own arm, simulating stroking the other person. (You know the message: "I'm not paying much attention to you, but I really am.") Then comes the climax: one person actually touches the other on the shoulder, the forearm, the wrist, or some socially acceptable (and available) body part. Normally the woman touches first, grazing her hand along her suitor's body in the most casual but calculated manner. One really lovely female whom I knew in California never seemed to be without partners, so I went with her to a singles' cocktail party just to observe her tactics. (Hey, life is my laboratory.) It turned out to be my **Aha!** moment in research. "What time is it?" she would purr throatily, leaning forward, and touching his watch-bearing wrist all the way around, gently, oh, so sexily. Subtle strokes no polite person could criticize. She danced every dance and if things got slow, she always asked a stranger the time. That girl had the best clockwork I have ever seen.

Human skin craves touching from birth to death – it is communication at a very deep level. So keep in mind the importance of touching when it comes to courting. Human skin, some say, can be compared to a field of grass, each blade a nerve ending so sensitive that the slightest graze can etch into the human brain an electric memory of the moment. The receiver notices this message instantly and imprints it on his brain permanently. If the receiver flinches or acts offended by the touch, the pickup is over. Halt. Stop. Finished. Kaput. If the receiver withdraws just a fraction of a second or a smidgen of an inch, the sender will generally not try again. We read "No-No" accurately. If the receiver smiles or returns the gesture in kind deliberately, even a teensy bit, a major barrier has been surmounted and the drama moves forward.

Sorry to bring you down to earth but most animals caress when courting. Watch all the courtship signals in the zoo. Our cousins, the chimpanzees, kiss, hug, pat, hold hands and daintily pick dandruff off each other and smack their lips at tasty morsels. Those acts signal "I care." Blue whales rub each other with their flippers. Male butterflies stroke and rub their loved one's abdomen as they couple. Dolphins nibble. Moles rub noses. Dogs lick. Cats rub and purr. Humans undoubtedly do animals one better. While I don't advise abdomen rubbing or such brazen stuff, it is interesting to watch human couples dance and then mentally compare people movements to animals' movements in the zoo, if you catch my meaning. I swear I've seen seen humans imitate everything from dolphin to mole behavior, but moving to a musical beat. Hint: best leave the dandruff-picking alone at the first meeting if you plan to make a good first impression, humanly speaking, that is.

Touch has been called the mother of the senses, and so it is. Every culture has touching codes regarding who, when, where, and even how. As do periods of history. When Anne of Green Gables was helped into the carriage by Gilbert Blythe, Marilla was shocked. Tsk, Tsk .A boy touching a girl on the pretext of courtesy. Fie. Shame. Today's kids wouldn't even know what we're talking about, etiquette rules have changed so much. Now we say don't touch any part of the other person's body that is generally covered by a bathing suit for a first meeting. That's a first impression etiquette requisite. Don't ask me about the second meeting, I'm still trying to figure that one out.

STAGE FIVE - KEEPING TIME: BODY SYNCHRONY

This is the final and most intriguing component of the initial meeting. As potential lovers become comfortable, <u>they pivot or swivel until their shoulders become aligned, their bodies positioned face-to-face</u>, forehead facing forehead at a social distance. This is real face-to-face confrontation where all points of nonverbal communication such as facial expression, eye behavior, and mouth movements may be closely observed. While abdomens probably are not touching, think of it in that context. (If butterflies need confrontation, then so do humans.) At first our couple moves in tandem just a bit at a time, then they move on with postural echoes that signal nonverbally stronger identification with each other. He will pick up a drink, she lifts hers. When he crosses his legs, she crosses hers; he leans left, she leans right, becoming a mirror image of him. They move in perfect rhythm, UNCONSCIOUSLY. Human mirroring begins in infancy, mimicking one's role model or parent. We mirror someone else when we feel comfortable with them. Please note: American women generally initiate the courting sequence starting with the subtle nonverbal cues we reviewed earlier. In case studies, women began 2/3 of all the pickups witnessed. When questioned later, the women were quite aware of having coaxed a potential lover into conversation, touching him carefully here and there, enticing him with coquettish looks, flirting eye and mouth behavior, questions, compliments, and jokes. The little hussies. And then they probably giggled. The lesson is: women are great ice-breakers, they start the drama, coaxing it along, and enjoying appropriate results. So, girls, if you are sitting in the corner, waiting for him to make all the right moves, don't blame me if the gal next door walks off with the prize, body rhythms all atwitter. Icebreakers, in case you never noticed, are hot!

When considering synchrony, try to bring to mind images of couples dancing the tango. See how the dancers dip and glide, their bodies moving in exact rhythms to each other. They bend, they twist, they dip to the exotic beat and that's synchrony. Ahhhh, synchrony.

28

CHAPTER SIX - THE EYES

"Jeepers creepers, where'd you get those peepers,
Jeepers creepers ,where'd you get those eyes?"

Your eyes can fetch you your lover, believe it or not. Many singles, when questioned, said the first item they checked in the body language of the other person is the eyes. Those baby blues, or whatever the hue. The eyes are not only the receivers of information; but serve as the transmitters of information as well. If you plan to fall in love one of these days, eyes will be the gatekeepers of your emotional state and the conductors of the transaction.

When we meet a stranger, we check out his eyes that clue us into his mood, availability, and yes, even his value system. Eyes tell us if you are alive (I'm not kidding Have you ever seen dead fish eyes on someone?), if you're intelligent, if you are kind, if you're interested in me, etc. *Ad infinitum.*

Eye contact is a magical moment in time when my eyes meet yours openly and then we decide if we want to go on mutually from there. The pupils accompanied by the colorful iris are set against the white of the eye. That white area is the dramatic backdrop which reveals the status-of-health. We check out the whites and then go back to pupil-to-pupil perusal. Eye contact also establishes the starting point of our relationship, ruling conversation etiquette. In order to avoid both of us speaking at the same time, the eyes act as traffic cops. I look at you and you look at me and then I speak. I speak and then look away. Now it's your turn to look at me, speak, and then look away. See how the eyes are regulators of information? If you won't play by the eye rules (and there are some strange souls out there who won't), plan to be discarded rapidly. Eye etiquette omnipotently rules that critical first impression.

If the other person is physically challenged in some way, eye behavior is critical for a successful first impression. When in a wheel chair, I found most strangers avoided eye contact with me. When on crutches (hey, I'm a klutz), people seemed ill at ease when they occasionally looked at me. They would look at anything but my infirmity, a broken leg. Watch your eye contact with someone who is infirm: give him good strong eye contact, polite words, and a smile. Perhaps you remember the story about J. P. Morgan, the billionaire who possessed a nose that resembled a gigantic strawberry due to some rare disease. From all reports, it was a sight to behold, and he was extremely sensitive about it. A little girl living in a swank Fifth Avenue mansion was coached carefully by her mother so that when she took tea with Mr. Morgan, she would be the epitome of grace and charm. While serving Mr. Morgan his cup of tea, and handing out the lumps of sugar, she carefully enunciated, "One nose or two, Mr. Morgan?" Back to task.

In order to keep the budding relationship growing, you need to look at the other person's face for roughly three-quarters of the time, utilizing glances that last 1-7 seconds. So those of you who stare at the ceiling or your shoes during a conversation are losing the game miserably. Keep glancing at the other person, probably about a second in time, but keep the ball bouncing. If you do not play the eye game correctly, you'll lose on the final score.

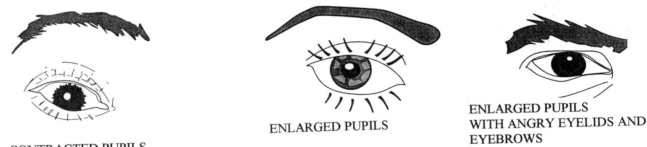

CONTRACTED PUPILS

ENLARGED PUPILS

ENLARGED PUPILS WITH ANGRY EYELIDS AND EYEBROWS

Do you know your pupils signal interest? If they are beautifully enlarged, making bedroom eyes, they signal affirmative reception. When the pupil is contracted into a tiny spot, disinterest is conveyed. Oh, yes, sorry to report that you cannot consciously control those pupils and their size. You cannot control sweating or skin tone either, so give up trying -- nature still controls certain signals whether you like it or not. It's about this time that someone in my seminars asks about the size of pupils and their relationship to light. Yes, light does control pupil size, as you know when you stand in bright sunlight having your picture taken, so try to choose critical spots where light is kind to your pupils, allowing them to enlarge beautifully such as in dimly lighted rooms.

Have you ever met someone who just will not give you eye contact, no matter how hard you try to get interaction? Either they are consciously manipulating the meeting, or they have a deep psychological problem you do not need in your life. People who will not look at us make us very uncomfortable, and who needs discomfort in a world already too uncomfortable. Eye contact is sometimes too emotionally charged for some people to handle. We can tolerate that reluctance once in a while but not for life, so be forewarned: eyes are telling great, deep-sounding truths.

If the other person's eye behavior disturbs you, pay attention to your instincts. Your body (heart, brain, brawn, and so on) is talking and you had best heed the message. I can cite a couple of times in my life when I did not obey my initial "instincts" and paid a heavy price for such stupid rebelliousness. God gave you a message system to pay attention to, so don't be foolish and risk future happiness for your derring-do; such audacity will win no orchids later. Do give thanks for your powers of subconscious perception and cherish and nurture them. Often our lover is first recognized by our faculty of intuition long before the slower brain begins to comprehend.

Let's explore negative eye behavior some more, such as icy killer's eyes or cold snake eyes. These are the eye movements we are inclined to stay away from and it pays to keep that *dictum* in mind. Then, too, we do not like a long unblinking stare. The chimpanzee-type hostile stare that is protective of one's territory is designed to frighten us. There **is** such a thing as an evil stare with harsh piercing eyes those evil eyes are not just in folklore. Another eye behavior that is negative is too many rapid blinks. (Sometimes allergies dry out pupils, and one must blink in order to moisten the eye.) Rapid blinks sometimes signal anger or nervousness. Study the context of the situation in order to figure out the reason for the rapid blinking, and then draw conclusions. If a stare is accompanied by a vertical frown line between the eyebrows, we become very alert. That fellow frightens us, and we become defensive. If the long gaze is accompanied by tiny contracted pupils, it is received as negative eye behavior and is definitely not the eye behavior you want in a lover. Another point we pick up nonverbally, which disturbs us, is when someone plainly does not want to look at us. This literally rattles our cages and all negotiations stop right there. That disturbing person stares over our heads or looks at other people <u>but not us</u>. I've been known to use this with audiences when there's one person who makes raucous comments, ruining my show. My display of disdain disturbs the disturber (noisy drunks who are adept at making wisecracks) until some bouncer ejects them from the conclave. As long as you're eye-detecting, how do you spot a liar? (Hey, I'm out to protect you!) One way, of course, is through his eyes. Pupil signals are involuntary, so a liar cannot control the size of his pupils no matter how hard he huffs and puffs. Statements accompanied by contracted pupils are often a sign of the liar. Liars know this quite often, so they try to hide their eyes from view in as many ways as possible. Dark glasses. Visors. Hands covering the eyes. Liars want you to read their eyes, but cleverly attempt to hide your own from scrutiny.

In the Middle Ages, Italians used the drug belladonna to enlarge the pupils of women artificially in order to look more beautiful, but its use is discouraged these days. We still enhance the eyes with cosmetics, making them dark, enveloped in shadow, and mysterious. On the other hand, just to confuse you, bold looks into your eyes are another way a manipulator can try to outdo you, so be a wary detective. Any three-year-old knows these con tricks: we just get more adept at evasive eye behavior as we grow older.

So as you size up the stranger, keep coming back to his eyes. Glance at other variables, but don't stray too far from his eyes: they must be your focal point.

31

I find Oriental eyes the toughest to decipher: slightly closed, impassive, very little movement. Once a high-powered CEO of a scientific organization hired me to go to an international convention of his industry. Out of thousands of people milling around in a huge convention hall, he challenged me to find the most powerful person in the group strictly using body language. Da da. In less than fifteen minutes I found him, a very quiet rotund Oriental gentleman, exuding tremendous power nonverbally. And I warned my client "If you do business with him, you'll lose your back teeth." Ruefully he rejoindered: " I have already have."

Occasionally I'm hired by romantic suitors who want me to check out their loved one before they ask the big question. I look before they leap, if you get my meaning. What's the first variable I check out? The eyes, the mirror of the soul, the reflectors of inner values. And I'm a tough checker so you can imagine how many candidates I have to turn down. Eyes: they tell all. Attorneys hire me to help choose juries and that must be accomplished in a small amount of time. What's the first variable I study? Eyes: they tell all.

Whatever the case, the way we look at another person tells the world how much we like them. If you are out to make friends, try to keep your eyes calm, steady, and willing to give eye contact as well as trade mutual gaze. We trade deep values in that critical mutual gaze.

When we are engaged in a conversation and are asked a question, we will often look at the questioner and then turn away, as if pausing to choose suitable words for an answer. Where we look is revealing, telling which side of the brain we're incorporating. If we turn to the right side, we tend to be scientific minded; if we turn toward the left, we tend to be more artistic or religious. The left hemisphere of the brain deals with verbal questions; the right half of the brain deals with spatial questions. So if I ask you how to spell a word, you use the left hemisphere of the brain; if I ask you where is the north direction from here, you'll use the right. Interesting.

Eyes can tell us who has the power and status in a conversation. Eyes can be snooty, staring down at the other person, sometimes accompanied by supercilious eyebrows haughtily lifted at the poor peasant. Who needs that person! Eyes can be inferior in demeanor, begging for some attention from a so-called superior person. Who needs eyes that beg like that! The person with the power will give longer glances; the subordinate person gives more glances, shorter in duration. Women tend to look more than men probably due to early childhood training. Visual dominance or visual subordination tell us a lot about how a person rates himself, and self-esteem is one variable to consider when choosing a lover.

We each need to affiliate in unique ways. Extroverts with their outgoing and sociable personalities tend to look at people more than introverts do. Extroverts enjoy the stimulation and emotional arousal that mutual gazes bring. Introverts, on the other hand, avoid uncomfortable public stirrings up, for they are retiring souls, loving privacy.

Cultures have different unwritten etiquette rules when it comes to eye behavior. Arab, Latino, and southern Europe, termed "contact cultures," stand closer to each other, touch more often, and tend to exchange more eye contact. (For the Arab culture, that's Arab male with male, please.) If you're from the cold climes, warm eye contact is difficult for you to handle. But do not, I repeat, <u>do not</u> judge warm eye behavior as insincere, dishonest, or impolite. It's just their way -- different than yours, but not necessarily better or worse.

What are the eyes we like? Those that look at the world calmly, not darting frantically all over the room like busy bees sipping nectar greedily. Those that give eye contact confidently. Those that look at us in a friendly style. Those that look as though the muscles surrounding the eye are relaxed, not taut nor frowning. Eyes that blink at regular intervals, not staring without any blinks like a fish.

We have preferences on iris color also. The darker the iris, the more the eye is judged beautiful. Sorry, you light-eyed folk, you'll just have to try harder. Seriously, light-eyed women can enhance those pale irises with eye makeup, and I don't know what to tell light-irised gentlemen. Dark eyes are considered sensuous and that's without even trying, doggone it! Tests have proved that photos of light-irised people were judged so-so, but when the irises of the photos were darkened, results came out much more favorably. Contact lenses help only to a certain degree, so keep praying for magic eye pills, I guess, you pale eyed folk.

LIGHT IRIS   DARK IRIS

How else can I tell if someone likes me after we've met for the first time? When they can't keep their eyes off me (almost as though the eyes are imitating hands). When they keep returning to my face, glancing away for a second, and them come right back to look at me again. Their eye behavior tells me they view me as a winner. It's very tough trying not to look at someone if they are interested in us. Eyes that gaze at us often and for a long duration <u>accompanied by large pupils</u> signal deep feeling and sincerity, and is highly flattering. So if someone keeps giving us "the eye," they are literally signaling their total interest. Females often accompany this eye behavior with nervous giggles and fluttery hand movements, betraying emotional investment also. And Latino ladies add an extra fillip with their mesmerizing fan motions.

Ah yes, a last briefing on eyes. When you smile, they appear warmer and more inviting. When you frown, they can be cold as ice. Got the picture? On with our exciting detective work!

Famous courtesans in history are always described partly because of their spellbinding eye behavior. Countless volumes are written about how they fixed the suitor with a rapt gaze that could not be broken even in an earthquake. These fascinating females are praised for their steady gazes, an unbroken attention span, undetected breaths, poise, and calm demeanor. The male subject's reaction? He laps up her eye message that say he is mah-ve-lous, darling. It holds just as true today.

BEAUTIFUL EYES

What kind of eyes do you want to present to a stranger? Rested, calm, healthy, trustworthy. Get enough sleep so the whites are pristine as possible. (Any illnesses that tint the white of the eye need medical attention, of course.) Keep your eye glances steady, not roaming and darting everywhere. Give good strong eye contact. If you hate looking at people, plan on losing your potential loved one: you will not appear trustworthy without direct eye contact.

Women can adorn their eyes with cosmetics, which enhances the eye message immeasurably. If you must wear eyeglasses, which disguise part of your eye message, make sure we can see all the eyeball and as much of the eyebrow as possible. Do not wear mirrored sunglasses indoors and expect polite reception. Tinted eyeglasses can give a downcast appearance to the facial expression, so try to stay as bright and open as possible.

At regular intervals check out your eyes in photographs and videotapes. Keep abreast of any eye changes that may be taking place so you can be, as they say, "on the cutting edge."

CHAPTER SEVEN - FACIAL EXPRESSION

Reading the other person's face and all its range of expressions started when you were a baby, so you should be pretty adept at this point in time in reading the following standard basic facial expressions as they range over the other person's face: Quick identification of the basic facial expression will help you center in on the subject's overriding emotion at the moment. These six facial expressions are considered universal. Try to memorize them so that you can clue in on the stranger rapidly.

HAPPINESS

The mouth smiles; eyes are relaxed or neutral with lower lids pushed up in lower face and that action thus bags the lower lids, causing the eyes to be narrowed. The outer corners of the lips are raised and often drawn back. There is no distinctive brow-forehead appearance worthy of note.

SADNESS

Eyebrows are drawn together with inner corners raised and outer corners lowered or level, or the brows are drawn down in the middle and slightly raised at the inner corners. The eyes seem glazed, with drooping upper lids and lax lower lids, or the upper lids are tense and pulled tightly at the inner corner, and down at the outer corner. The mouth is either open with partially stretched trembling lips, or closed with the outer corner pulled slightly down.

SURPRISE

Here the eyebrows are sharply raised and curved accompanied by long horizontal forehead lines. The eyes are wide open; the dropped wide-open mouth with parted lips shows no stress or tension. The general signal is that of genuine astonishment.

FEAR

The eyes and mouth really get a workout on this one with raised and drawn-together brows, short horizontal or vertical forehead wrinkles, and the corners of the mouth are drawn back, with the lips stretched. The mouth may or may not be open. Eyes are opened with tension showing in lower lids.

ANGER

Angry eyes can scarcely be missed: brows pulled down, with forehead wrinkles sometimes curved are centered above the eyes. The upper eyelids appear to be lowered, and the lower eyelids are tensed and raised in a squinting fashion. The lips are tightly pressed together or open, and the mouth is often positioned in a curious squared fashion.

DISGUST

Sometimes confused with anger, look for brows drawn down but not pulled together with wrinkles showing on the bridge of the nose. Lower eyelids are pushed up and raised, but not tensed. Deep creases run from the wrinkled nose to the open mouth with upper lips raised (almost in a sneer) and the lower lip pushed forward. Sometimes the mouth is closed with the upper lip pushed up by the raised lower lip.

Your brain controls your facial expressions and different parts of the face control different expressions. Some cultures display emotions facially more than others. The British so-called "stiff upper lip" coolly restricts certain facial expressions easily displayed by other cultures. The British get a bum rap on this one, for several cultures in the Western world, especially the Teutonic, are also cool. If the person you are surveying is Oriental, reared in a traditional fashion of the Far East, expect a suppression of facial expression. Geographically, Americans have different facial expression displays. New England is considered the coolest and most guarded, and the Sunbelt's vividly facile displays of emotions show in various facial movements.
As you meet the stranger, it is important that you look at him/her directly, displaying a pleasant facial expression yourself. Now check out his face and all its components. Here is where you need to incorporate facial scrutiny. Glass suggests the following steps:

1- Look at the person's entire face for two seconds.
2- Next, look at his eyes for two seconds.
3- Move your gaze to the nose, mouth, and chin – looking at each for two seconds.
4- Now, go back and glance at the entire face for two seconds.
5- Repeat Steps 1-3 throughout the conversation.
6- Always attempt to determine the general emotion behind that facial expression.
7- Is this person shy? Petulant? Pouting? Dissatisfied? Anxious? Unreceptive? Downright hostile? Or, are the fates with you and all the variety of facial expressions positive, open, warm, friendly? Experiment. Sample. Keep looking and assessing.

Facial expression detection will aid you greatly in sizing up the other person, and if you read correctly, will steer you in the right direction. Faces: they are wonderful!

CHAPTER EIGHT - COLOR

Color can make or break that first impression. It can make you attractive and vibrant or certain unflattering tones can make you look as dead as a doornail. It's your choice, so from this point on, for the rest of your life, wear only your own most flattering shades. Color influences our love choice in manifold ways and it also rules our moods in manifold modes, so screw your head on tight for this chapter and make wise color choices accordingly. Yes, the advice applies to both genders.

God gave you three natural colors that form the artistic canvas for your own personal flattering range of hues. Those colors are found in your eyes, skin, and hair. You can fool with them all you want, but if we study you carefully, we can still perceive what natural colors God gave you despite contact lenses, hair dye, cosmetics, *ad infinitum*. Work with these natural tints; do not attempt to distort them unfavorably. (You know, such as a woman of 60 just does not have coal black hair naturally, movie stars to the contrary, unless some hair fairies have wrought miracles upon milady's beautiful head.)

Woman uses color more widely and boldly than does the male, just the opposite from the animal world. Since men have a narrower color range, especially professionally, they must make wise varieties of choices sparingly. This chapter should give you accurate clues as to what colors will enhance your own life.

Some people are color blind when choosing colors for themselves. Get yourself a couple of dozen color chips from the local paint store that you can use for clothing, home, car, and accessory choices. If your skin, hair, and eyes match clear pastels suitably, then stick to that color spectrum. (Paints and books sometimes call this System I.) Some of us have murkier skin, eyes, and hair, so we need shades that have a little grey or brown tones added for flattery. (These darker hues are called System II.) Position yourself in front of a bright window with a large hand mirror and start matching those color chips to your skin, eyes, and hair. If needed, find a discerning soul to help you. Now you are beginning to find flattering tones to use for a long time to come. Take those chips with you when you make purchases because fluorescent lighting in stores is artificial and absolutely no help at all when it comes to seeing yourself realistically.

"Okay, " you say, "cut to the chase. What colors make me lovable or sexy?" Here we go:
Generally, people show a color preference for blues and greens over yellows, reds, and oranges when studies are conducted. Women show a slight preference for red over blue, men to blue over red when giving a red/blue decision. Orange is preferred to yellow by men, and yellow to orange by women. For both groups greenish-yellow (chartreuse) is one of the least like of the

chromatic colors, but is big for style choice in the last years of this waning century. Tests conducted with college students index that red, yellow, and orange are associated with excitement, stimulation, and aggression; blue and green are associated with calm, security, and peace; black, brown, and gray are associated with melancholy, sadness, and depression; yellow is associated with cheer, gaiety, and fun; and purple is associated with dignity, royalty, power and sometimes even sadness. The warm end of the spectrum is red and gold; the cool colors incorporate either blue or green.

Thus, we know if you are a woman, and want to please a man wear the following colors:

MEN'S FAVORITE COLORS

Blue (Wedgewood or Baby Blue the best)
Orange
Sweetheart Pink (Bolder than Baby Pink)
Peach
Violet

If you are a man and want to please a woman with your choice of colors, wear <u>touches</u> of:

WOMEN'S FAVORITE COLORS
Red
Yellow
Bold Blue (Cobalt)
Bright Green (Kelly)
Purple

As you can see, men like women in softer, more feminine shades that reveal them as more pliable and appealing. Women prefer men to wear touches of bolder colors, asserting their masculine strength and even a bit of male vigor. Women need to beware of wearing too much of a bold color (all red or all purple, for instance), because this can be interpreted as threatening and too aggressive. (Rapunzel is never depicted as a bold hussy clothed in a scarlet dress. Madonna, on the contrary, in her tartish, pre-madre days wore red or black boldly and looked like a very B-A-A-A-D woman calculatedly.)

If you are a meek or timid person, touches of red will imbue your being with boldness. If you feel frustrated or defeated in some way, yellow or red will pick up your spirits. If you tend to be an Oscar the Grouch, pink or peach will make you happier. (Raspberry pink will make you hungry, so beware which pink you pick.) The bolder the color you wear, then the bolder you appear. People who love soft pink tend to be gentle souls who are often dilettantes; lovers, not fighters. If you are a warm, sociable person, orange will please you. Good natured people love to sport orange, but often orange lovers remain happily single, thus take care lest you send off the wrong signals by wearing too much orange. If you feel weak in the intellectual department, wear yellow. It's a great brain picker-upper. If your energy is low, wear yellow. Color affects energy, health, weight, moods, and most importantly for your task, approachability.

Color is powerful, sending forth psychological messages almost anyone can interpret. For instance, one seldom finds sugar or beauty products packaged in brown; brighter colors such as blue or green convey sweetness. Red increases energy; orange and Kelly green give us joy; yellow speeds up movement; the green of nature gives us balance; turquoise gives us immunity; cobalt blue (so the Irish believe) gives protection; Wedgewood blue lends calmness; violet imbues us with gentle dignity; purple gives us image power; and black makes us glamorous, sinister, or an authority figure. Take your choice. Bright red can increase blood pressure, respiration, and the pulse, while a soft shade of blue can have just the opposite effect. The power messages of color go on and on exponentially.

Master Lin Yun, probably the world's greatest color scientist around these days, teaches that color influences our lives in four ways. Use these points for your own attire, your environment, and cosmetics or facial adornments. These are the best definitions of the importance of color I've ever seen"

1- Color defines for us what exists and what does not exist.
2- Color discloses the status of one's health and fortunes.
3- Color inspires emotion.
4- Color structures our behavior.

Some Color Caveats: If you are accustomed to wearing colors such as all grey, beige, or taupe, expect to be overlooked part of the time. Thus, men who wear drab colors had best think of bright ties, pocket handkerchiefs, sweaters, or even socks if they want to be noticed. Europeans, particularly the French, wear neutrals almost always but they smarten the color up with tasteful adornments, expensive materials, and superb classic design. If your skin is pale and also your clothes, you may appear sickly, so attempt to wear colors that imbue you with vitality.

Wear appropriate colors: too bold or garish may not look right at a dignified, formal occasion. (Can you see Henry Kissinger in a purple shirt at the White House? What's he doing in the White House anyway?) If we know red creates pent-up emotions, I don't advise wearing a whole outfit of red to peace talks in Bosnia or Palestine. Orange is the all-time least favorite color - throughout the world, so I would not advise it for a wedding dress or baby's layette. When your *ch'i* (vital energy) is up, wear bright colors to match; when an occasion is somber, wear appropriate hues. It is said the highest intellects prefer green, the gentle green of nature. Green-wearers are definitely loners, preferring solitude to a crowded existence.

If you are going into a situation that fills you with anxiety, what color will cheer you, hearten you, and fill you with additional energy? Red. Nice bright red. Not burgundy or wine red with a bluish tinge: just a bright red with a tinge of orange. Red.

Hopefully, this chapter leaves strong lessons for you. Examine your colors and their usage in these categories of your life. Jot in as many notes as you feel are relevant to you now and in the future.

Home

       Living Room
       Exterior
       Bedroom
       Kitchen
       Bathroom

Work

       Office
       Reception Area
       Workroom
       Washroom

Car
       Exterior
       Interior

Wardrobe (Predominant colors)
       Coats, Outer Garment
       Professional Attire
       Casual Attire
       Formal Attire (dates, dances, parties, etc.)
       Sleep Wear
       Shoes

CHAPTER NINE - GENDER

The gender difference between men and women, so they say, amounts to about a piddling three percent. But that three percent is a tremendous amount when we look at its effects all about us. This chapter is about those salient differences and how we pick up on them in far less than a minute nonverbally. Gender is a prominent variable in the first encounter.

Whatever your gender preference and your own identification, this chapter is written as broadly as possible, taking in as many lifestyles as possible. Bear with me if I've missed somebody: I'm trying to include everybody and his or her life style openly.

We zoom in on gender behavior from the very beginning as you singles well know. Does he move and act with masculine bearing? Does she give forth the aura of charming femininity? In other words, does he come across as a man? Is she instantly recognizable as a woman? These questions may seem silly, but my years of research prove to me that all negotiations stop until we can ascertain clearly the gender identification of the other person. I once stood at a glove counter in Beverly Hills when Clark Gable came up to purchase a mundane pair of gloves for himself. Up came a woman customer with the same intent, and spying Mr. Gable right there beside her, fainted dead away. "This happens to me all the time," he muttered, looking annoyed and embarrassed. Hmm. His masculinity must have been a real problem to social success for him, poor darling. I can't think of another male who gave off the magnificent aura of rugged manliness as he did, and I suspect he didn't even work at it. Just natural talent. There was, in any instance, no mistaking his gender. The devil in me wonders what would have happened had the scene been played at the underwear counter. Fie on me.

Gender display is the way we exhibit our sexual identity to the world. The site of the fig leaf humans wear in paintings is called the Taboo Zone and for women that fig leaf also includes the bust. This Zone is a curiously sensitive area of the body: one must not overtly stare at it, and yet one is constantly aware of it covertly We call that subtle glance Civil Inattention -- we pretend not to see, yet we don't miss a trick. No pun intended.

To be caught staring at male genitals is a no-no for women, and how well I know it. I told you before that life is a laboratory but sometimes the scientist in me gets me in big trouble. There I was in Denmark, in the Copenhagen railroad station, minding my own business, acting like a lady. Suddenly, coming toward me was a middle-aged male genitalia display, brazenly sported through transparent white silk pants by a good looking wretch. He laughed when he caught me looking, the old goat. I was red-faced, outright mortified, and he was delighted that he'd caught me sneaking a peek. Rats. We have taboos about looking at the Taboo Zone too openly, don't forget. One church I attended had a handsome young minister who loved to bike ride in those tight fitting one piece latex outfits. They hide no sin, are tighter than skin, those garments, and his masculinity, while rubberized, was prominently displayed. You've guessed it, I got caught again. I now attend church where ministers are eighty if they are a day and generally wear three-piece suits. My eyes are now better behaved.

Since time immemorial, men have had their maleness and women their femaleness in image display. The two are worlds apart. And, as the French say, *"Vive la diffe'rence!"* We're not talking political power here, we are talking sexual identity. If a woman likes being a female, she conveys that message silently in her pleasant facial expression, her direct eye contact, her erect head and carriage, her firm steps, and even her attire announce that she is a woman, doggone it, so look alert. The same goes for the man. In an easy, affable air, he lets us all know he is a fellow who is at ease with himself and his masculinity.

Unisex, androgyny, is all around us and no doubt will grow stronger in the future, but right now we have two basic sexes and individual variations thereof. The future holds tantalizing peeks at gender displays and their 21st Century variations, and hopefully, more respect for individuality.

That three per cent sexual difference demands our attention constantly. The media, the marketplace, the office -- you name it -- all display the two sexes dancing around each other, sounding and sniffing each other out every bit as much as the animal world.

The differences between the male and the female are many. Women's bodies have a layer of fat beneath the skin that is seductive to the male when he views its dimpled, touchable beauty. Women have babylike features suggesting a girlish immaturity. They generally have a smaller body than the male, a thinner neck, narrower shoulders, smoother skin which has far less hair than her male counterpart, shorter legs, and a more pronounced pelvic girdle that produces a unique "awkward" gait. But, oh, how men are attracted to that gait. Men's bodies can run more easily, are larger, hairier and heavier, sport larger noses, larger jaws, harder facial lines, and beards. Men's muscles are larger, as is his skeleton, when compared to the female. He is considered *macho* the stronger he is built; she is considered feminine the daintier she looks.

Men and women decipher each other as they size up the other's sexual components residing below the neck. Men look at the female figure first, then take a second or two to look at the face, then size up the bust and hips, not skipping the Taboo Zone. That's a lot of quick roaming with the eyes. Finally he goes back to the facial area, checking out the eyes and then the facial expression and once again back to the "orbs," the breasts, the rounded shoulders, and lastly, the genitalia, including the derriere. (All these are rounded in shape, thus "orb.") I've seen photos where, knees pulled up to the chin, the knees take on a cute orbed sexual connotation also. The male will take in almost incidentally such fine points as the quality of her hair, the softness and smoothness of her skin, the slimness of her ankle, her hand shape,--all those fine points that make her special, but are really secondary in his major survey. He's pretty straightforward, almost businesslike, in making a gender assessment of her. Watch men at parties and see how fast they size up a new female. They run through their inventory list of likes and dislikes rapidly

42

and are fairly open in their viewing. Who said men don't like to shop?

Not so she, when she's into sizing up him. First, she spends some time looking at his eyes, his eyelids, his eyebrows. Then she surveys hands, his height, his shoulders, his "buns," and along the way surreptitiously takes in his Taboo Zone. She's not as straightforward in her scrutiny nor as fast as he. She tends to be embarrassed if caught looking , thus she scrutinizes covertly.

Men generally classify themselves as "breast men" or "leg men" or whatever, but often they spend considerable time looking at milady's waist. The hourglass figure has been around some forty thousand years and the small waist will no doubt be favored for a long time to come. If her waist is 15% smaller than her hips, he's tickled pink. 15% is a winner!

Let's take a look at what the genders prefer, according to Givens:

MEN PREFER
Attractive Figure (Chest, Waist, Hips, Legs)
Sexy Orbs (Shoulders, Breasts, Derriere)
Pretty Face
Smooth Skin
A Well-Turned Ankle
Shape of Hand
Luster of Hair

WOMEN PREFER
Eyes (Crinkles in Corners, Lower Eyelid Fold)
Sexy Eyes(Deep-set with Long Dark Lashes)
Eyes That Look At Me A Long Time
Hands
Height
Nice Shoulders
Energy
Buns

"Thus, men inventory a woman's tangible body cues, tally them off item by item, and then judge her physical charm on a scale of one to ten," says David Givens. Do women use the same cues? What a surprise -- they don't. Rather, they read the subjective signals of the masculine character under scrutiny; and they neither reflexively mentally disrobe nor jump into bed with unfamiliar

43

men. Her subjectively interpreted signals have little to do with lovemaking *per se*; women make a relationship personal first and sexual second. Men, on the other hand, reverse the process and see women's features in a harsh, <u>erotic</u> light. Temperament comes only **after** they've sized up the potential for lovemaking. First things first, that's the pragmatic male style. There's that difference again, so key your scrutiny to the opposite gender. If you are a male in this drama, don't rush. If you're a female, don't dawdle.

Whichever gender we scan, when you see the chest or pelvis (or both!) thrust forward boldly, almost as though flaunted, recognize this as the most important gender display of all. That old Taboo Zone is omnipotent when it comes to capturing our attention.

<u>SOME GENDER DIFFERENCES</u>

<u>HE</u>	<u>SHE</u>
Muscular Neck	Longer, thinner neck
Prominent voice box	No Adam's apple showing
Thicker, more muscular shoulders	Rounded (orbed) shoulders
Thick, muscular arms	Narrow feminine arms
Flat chest	Full-breasted chest
Broad, thick fingers	Longer, thinner fingers
Larger volumed rib cage	Shallower, less muscled chest
Thicker waist	Thinner waist; 15% smaller than hips
Full-sized buns	Rounder, fatter derriere

The tasteful manner in which we display or hide the Taboo Zone has much to do with that initial encounter's reception. Rock stars who enlarge the appearance of the crotch by stuffing socks in their Taboo Zones are rated tasteless by some sensitive people. (Of course, someone is paying them huge sums of money, but let's deal with middle class America here – the kind of people you socialize with.). Women who show off tasteless cleavage at inappropriate times do not rate favorably with men who are looking for a more refined lady. Today 's short skirts are a real test for women who want to look as though they know the meaning of "well bred." Take a look at the late night talk shows and observe how female guests lower their bodies into a chair and the manner in which they remain seated. The challenging act of seating oneself can be graceful and elegant, or look like a come-hither gal at the local bar. And speaking of breeding, elegance, and all that refined stuff, The Queen, my dears, unlike Sharon Stone, never shows her unmentionables, or as she 'd probably refer to them: "private parts" when on public display. She sits on public platforms, climbs in and out of cars, and bends over to pat little tykes on the head, never once looking like a tramp. End of sermon.

Ever since an unflattering TV appearance in the Midwest, I always give a skirt the sitz test, seated in front of a mirror in the store before purchasing a dress. I imagine the mirror to be the camera and then try to see what the camera sees. I'd hate to tell you what that mirror reveals if one is not alert. Do you suppose Queen Elizabeth II gives her garb the same test?

Guard yourself against gross gender displays. Try seating **yourself** in front of a mirror, as I'm forced to do, and rate yourself on a scale of one to ten on how graceful and elegant you look. Check that fanny to be sure it is not too prominent. Standing posture is revealing as well. Zunin says we reveal gender while standing, and he refers to it as "vertical sex." This is not a position in which to enjoy sex sleazily, but means simply that as we stand, we reveal our sexual overtones in that encounter. "Vertical sex," says Zunin, "is foreplay begun with the eyes as well as the hands and body. We respond visibly to visual appreciation." You know what Zunin means. A stranger lets me know, nonverbally, that I am attractive in gender display, that he wants to know me better, and I probably give the same sexual feedback. Body language sexual shopping. Just looking, just mentally testing. We each understand when someone appreciates our sexual identity; and as our nonverbal response whets interest, subsequent communication leads to ACT TWO.

Observe gender display all about you and learn what is successful and appropriate, then look at the other end of the spectrum. Unsuccessful gender display all too frequently results in sad human interest stories.

Try to see the genders on an equal basis when it comes to power and status. If you're a male of the old fashioned school who sees men superior to women, you're gonna have a lot of trouble dealing with today's women, especially if you're looking for the gal to share your life, your lunch, and your home. I see too many men (usually over 40, but there are some young fossils out there also) who do not understand why they are not successful when looking for a partner. Yet, when I check out their body language, I see disdainful facial expressions, supercilious eyebrows that look like a titled English lord snootily surveying the peasant, sometimes a sneer, and even narrowed eyes, up-tilted nose, and out-thrust chin sometimes accompanied by a snobbish sniff -- all denoting prejudice. He's not about to share power or status with her. These gentlemen are conveying nonverbally a bias against females, regarding them obviously as inferior. Gals, if you take up with this type of jaundiced guy, expect trouble. Pay attention to all those body language signs that are speaking loudly to you.

Men, the same goes for you. If she seems haughty, cold, self-centered, like a cool princess in the castle tower, please beware. Some females act as though you are favored if they deign to pay attention to you. That type of woman expects you to be her personal body servant, awaiting her beck and call. If you pick up these signals on the initial encounter, you'd be very wise to keep shopping for another lady fair. The cold princess will probably be nothing but trouble.

Look for the person who is open, friendly, and well-balanced. If they're too giddy, back off. If they're too sour, disappear. If they're critical, who needs them. Look for all the negative signals you can find, and then be smart. Try to imagine this type person opposite you at the breakfast table, making carping remarks, and I expect you'll be out the door in less than a minute.

Age can be a barrier also. Some subjects do not seem comfortable with their own age, seeking a parent or child figure. Oh, we sometimes see lovely young things pairing up with a fellow the age of her grandfather, but I figure she needs a good IQ exam. "And," say I, "there looks like a wonderful relationship that will last at least a year." Ha. You know. Try to look your age, act your age, and be graceful about it – and this goes for any age from 20 to 100.

Whatever your persuasion, look for someone with whom you can easily share the rest of your life. Harmony should be your goal. Peace. Contentment. Mutual loving. Kindness. Respect.

What we're looking for is an ideal situation where each gender has respect for the other. Without mutual respect, we ain't got much.

CHAPTER TEN - SPACE

Make space your treasured working tool when searching for your Significant Other. Those who ignore the magic of territoriality live to regret their ignorance, so use this chapter wisely. Proxemics is the study of the use of space, an important ingredient to monitor when looking for one's heart's darling. You must begin to learn how distance affects the impressions we make because such knowledge tells us about social interactions. Distance tells us how personal our relationship is to one another as well as how cool or remote our interaction can be. Moving the distance between you and the other person closer can make the meeting more personal and friendly; further apart means the transaction is more impersonal. The closer the distance, the warmer our body language. It's that simple.

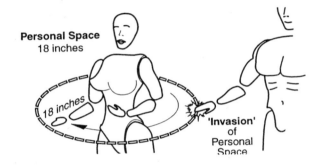

Have you ever moved too rapidly, gotten too close to the stranger, and unknowingly killed what could have been a budding romance? Or, on the other hand, have you stayed <u>too</u> remote and thus lost your quarry? Your unwise usage of space or territory lost you the game, so pay attention. When you misuse territory, you can offend the other person and end up being rejected. Wrong space usage will lose you the whole ball game. If you are rude or aggressive in your sharing of space with someone else, plan to have an unfriendly situation – <u>nonverbally.</u> Keep an eye on how you observe distances: it's a critical area to control.

Each of us has an invisible space bubble about eighteen inches from the body that marks our own private territory. That space bubble is my own sacred territory, and don't you forget it. Animals and humans become very territorial when their space is invaded uninvitedly. They growl and gnash if their space is invaded rudely. Humans are a little more subtle, but results are about the same as with our animal cousins. It is important for meeting etiquette and throughout all negotiations, that we respect the other person's personal space. The space bubble is surrounded by a barrier wall invisible to the naked eye, yet plainly marked by our body language protective stances. If, without nonverbal invitation, you do invade someone's personal space impolitely, beware of negative reception. Always make sure you are obtaining friendly <u>nonverbal</u> permission (probably from the eyes) before you enter someone's personal space. Invasion without permission equals unfriendly reception. Incidentally, these space *dicta* apply as well to people in wheel chairs, on crutches, or the elderly, and even the young.

When couples are in a close or intimate relationship, we can read the signs by their usage of space: they may share long gazes or sit closely to each other -- signaling a very warm relationship. Obviously, such close contact has been invited and permitted. Close approaches when not invited generally result in smoldering feelings revealed in open resentment. I boldly sat on the desk of a powerful executive in the aerospace industry just to test him and you could feel his negativity reach the boiling point almost immediately. When I picked up his favorite pen, and (still perched on his desk uninvitedly), leaned into his personal space, he boiled over, growling, "What the hell are you doing, Jackie?" I pointed out how often I'd observed his lack of respect for employees' personal spaces, in similar fashion to what I'd just pulled, and he sheepishly said, "Okay. Let's sign up your training. I guess I need it." I'd gotten into his personal zone, and then smoodged flagrantly into the space we label intimate. That's a No-No. I'd pushed my way from social distance into the intimate – uninvitedly. Again, the amount of space between us tells the world the kind of relationship we have:

FOUR DISTANCE ZONES

INTIMATE - Touching to 18 inches
    (Lovers making love; sports events, family members touching, intrinsic.)

PERSONAL - 18 inches to 4 feet
    (Touch more limited; body heat and odor are unnoticeable [usually]; can see more of the other person.)

SOCIAL - 4 feet to 12 feet
    (More formal exchanges; typical business dealings; visual cues more important.)

PUBLIC - 12 feet to larger spaces
    (Formal exchanges; calling across the street; cannot see much of facial expression.)

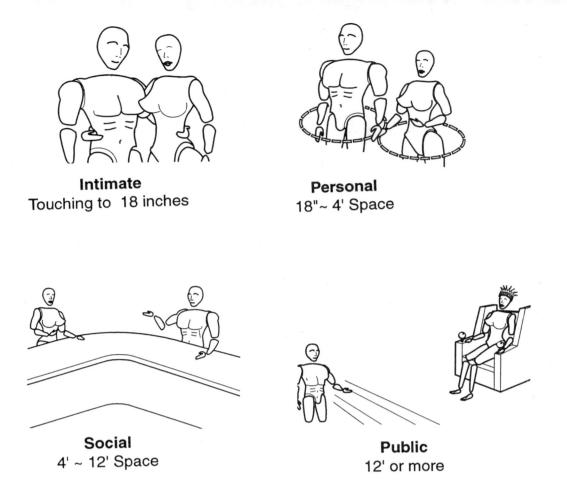

Intimate
Touching to 18 inches

Personal
18" ~ 4' Space

Social
4' ~ 12' Space

Public
12' or more

Check out social situations and see if you can tell what kind of relationship it is that you are observing. Then at the next event when you are looking for your love, observe your own behavior. Are you adhering to the unwritten etiquette of space behavior? Do you invade other peoples' space bubbles uninvitedly? Do you back up people, right against the wall if need be, and then note they don't seek you out? Do you stay in your allotted space at the dining table or do you invade other spaces just like a barbarian? Are you rude and selfish when it comes to space allotment? Watch yourself in check-out lines, in movie theatre seats, in driving on the highway, in finding a parking space, etc. If you are a space tyrant, expect negative results. We just don't like space hogs.

Now observe that other person and note their space etiquette. If it is too boorish, keep looking. There has to be a more polite soul out there for you.

49

CHAPTER ELEVEN - BODY LEANS

The way you hold your body can reveal your interests, your turn-offs, and even your sources of boredom. Your mama told you to sit up straight, but I think mama was wrong. She should have told you to lean forward. Crazy, eh? Like a fox.

Sit straight up in your chair, back not touching the chair at all. That's called a neutral position, and one I interpret as not positive, but negative. Sit way back in the chair, spine against the chair back. (You look as though the other person is a bad smell, to tell the truth.) That's **very** negative. Now lean forward, looking at the other person intently. Hurray, that's positive! If you accompany that forward lean with a warm facial expression, strong eye contact, and maybe even placing your hands forward, clasped on the knees or just folded, that's even more positive, showing signs of interest. As you lean toward him, maintain strong eye contact signaling, "I'm interested."

Do not go to a singles' event and lean against the wall or your chair, exhibiting a negative body lean. Expect nil in response from the other person with your spinal performance. Leaning forward requires some effort on your part, and that is how we interpret such posture -- putting forth some effort to receive sweet rewards.

A slumped posture with bent shoulders and concave chest indicates a loser. Lift that head, get the angle of the neck upward, lift the shoulders, make yourself as tall as possible for a winning posture. Straight tall posture, (no matter your actual height) are earmarks of a winner. If your slumped posture is accompanied by downcast eyes and a sad facial expression, plan to have a No-Win evening.

When we are interested, we unconsciously lean forward indicating an attitude of interest. I love audiences that lean toward me, give me warm eye contact, smile, and even offer affirming head nods. Then I know I'm on the right track.

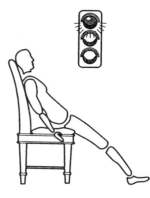 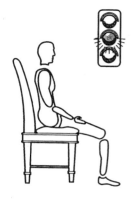 

Body Leans

Red light   (Stop) '   **Backward Lean**

Yellow light (Caution) ' **Neutral Lean**

Green light   (Go!) '   **Forward Lean**

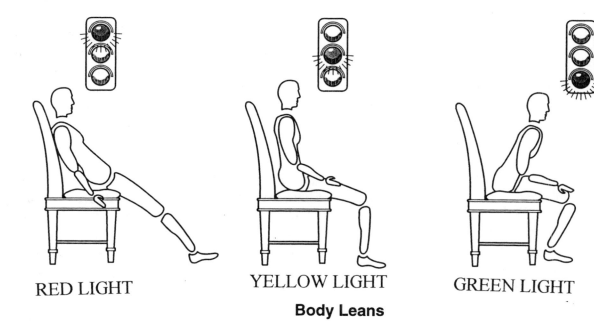

RED LIGHT   YELLOW LIGHT   GREEN LIGHT

Body Leans

CHAPTER TWELVE - GESTURES

Anything that moves from the trunk can gesticulate: the head, the arm and hands, the feet and legs. So check out your subject for all the movements from those parts of the body for emphasis and meaning. Gestures clarify meaning such as index finger pointing in order to magnify words, and head nods to give emphasis to certain words. Think of gestures as supplemental language.

When people are nervous, they tend to use gestures (particularly hands) too frequently. Be kind, do not judge the other person too harshly if he over-gesticulates on that initial impression. His overuse of gestures may just be stagefright.

The first type of gesture to take a look at is the Baton Gesture: movements that "dance" to the beat of our words. "Over there" we say, with a head nod or a pointing finger. "You are in trouble" accompanied by a face-forward jutting jaw thrust at your intended victim. "And another thing," the forefinger raised like a prophet of yore. "Listen to me" in synchrony with a tap on the other guy's shoulder. Baton Gestures accentuate the message dramatically.

Your intended will do the same thing. Maybe she'll brush lint of your collar. (Grooming you.) Perhaps she'll tap your wrist to emphasize speech utterances.

Too many gestures can be obstacles to successful interaction, so guard yourself against flailing the air with bold arm and hand gestures that detract from the calm leadership role you intend to assume. Avoid nervous gestures such as fussing with clothing, pulling at your hair, adjusting a collar or tie, and, yes, wringing your hands. Anxious signals such as these tell the world you're neither thinking nor behaving like a winner. Fold your hands quietly and when you do gesticulate, move slowly and deliberately, gesturing toward the other person, not yourself. Occasionally I find clients who can't seem to keep their heads still. The head can gesticulate emphatically, but we don't like it to see-saw so that we get seasick. Get a firm control of that neck and stop waggling your head around like a Japanese doll welcoming a shopper to a store.

Different cultures have different gestures, even involving rapidity and duration. Research studies conducted in New York with Italians and Jews, found that the two groups gestured more than other cultures. The Jewish style is termed "ideographic" the hands tracing thought patterns in the air. The Italians, on the other hand, use "physiographic" movements -- gestures that illustrate speech. Watch yourself in telephone conversations and note how often your illustrate your words with gestures even though your listener cannot possibly see a darned movement you're making. We can't help it -- we just must illustrate ideas with body movement.

Do not forget that your feet gesticulate also. On consultancy jobs I see inappropriate feet behavior constantly. Angry feet that stomp across the floor. Feet that are bored with a meeting and point to the door. Feet that like to play "footsie" with someone else's foot. Feet that jiggle.

Feet that swing either angrily or happily. Pigeon-toed feet that look wimpish. Aggressive feet that invade territory rudely. Feet that kick (and I never think it's in fun). Shy feet. Feet that indicate lack of balance. Feet that move with uncertainty. Tired feet. Sick feet. Check out your own feet, particularly as you walk, and you'll learn a great deal about your own equanimity.

I won't bore you with all the technical names for gestures, but please be aware they can indicate direction, they can beckon, bid farewell, and even threaten us. When you're looking at a potential partner, try to determine if they use soft gestures or harsh ones. Do their gestures move rapidly and perhaps agitatedly, or do their motions almost float delightfully like a piece of silk? Do they keep pointing to oneself or do they hold their hands in a palms-up movement? The palms-up is the sweetest hand gesture we can make and it's called "The Bowl." Use the bowl gesture whenever tempers are fraught and you will see an immediate cooling down of hostilities. Display the bowl gesture in courting and note the psychological results. You'll be pleased.

If all movements seem under control in a relaxed, easy fashion, the person you're scrutinizing is probably a sweetheart. If they keep pointing to themselves, you get the picture already. If their hand movements are tough and choppy, find someone else, please. Life is too short to have pain and *angst*-filled days.

Gestures may seem trivial, but they give insightful clues to the other person, if you care to take a look and then a very objective assessment. Ray Birdwhistell thinks gestures are a kind of linguistics, serving as metaphors for periods, commas, exclamation points, and so on. I'll agree with him, handily. (Sorry about that. I'll try to keep my paws off puns in the future.)

Incidentally, try to get a fix on your own use of gestures. Is there a home movie or a videotape of you in an informal setting where you can observe your hands, feet, and head nods? Play that tape over and over until you can decipher what type of movements you employ most frequently. You may note some gestures that are negative, so now is the time to clean up your act.

CHAPTER THIRTEEN - TOUCHING

Imagine falling in love and not being able to touch your lover. Seems impossible? It was the norm in days of yore and is still the rule in many parts of the world. Thank heavens we live here and now because for us touching is like spices used in cooking: a touch makes the dish taste deliciously better. In the Western world we do not really know the other person until we have (ahem) pressed the flesh, to borrow a phrase from our wily politicians, who know how to get to the heart of the matter quickly.

Think of the magical properties of touch in literature: the prince kisses Snow White and she awaken as his lips touch hers. Rhett sweeps Scarlett into his arms: the savage sensuous of his touch awakens her to a passion she had never experienced before. Heathcliffe shatters the window to lean out into the dark, cold, misty night to touch the ghost of Cathy: the touch of the living with the wraith of the dead. We touch the Bible when we swear an oath. The bridal couple clasps hands to signal their joint venture from this point on. It's everywhere we look, the pervasiveness of touching in our lives.

You're no stranger to touch, having touched mama's inner skin all the time you floated in her womb. The skin is our largest organ, covering and enveloping us in a protective, sensitive wrapper. That same skin totally involves us in gender awareness, falling in love, and making love. Touching communicates demonstrably in many ways. We can control the other person through touch: we can hurt them, soothe them, lend support, and yes, fall in love with them. That's why touching is included in this book -- it will aid you in your search for the love of your life. Touching is one of the most important variables in body language.

Will touch aid your first impression? In a word, immensely, if you use it correctly. The average woman receives twelve touches a day; the average male receives only eight. Whatever your gender, if you're with the majority of people, you enjoy being touched by the appropriate people in the right circumstances. Americans are not very big at touching, not as much as our Latino neighbors to the south, so you may have to rev up your touch motor to get it into operational speed.

Courtesy plays a big role in touching, so do not mess with etiquette rules regarding touch. Initially, only touch the other person's hand or shoulder. Hands off the knees, please, and no condescending pats on the head. Touching is a powerful unspoken language so you want to convey polite feeling, but not too high a dosage of friendliness. If you come on too strong in the beginning, particularly with touch, you'll end up losing the whole nine yards. Women generally can initiate touches more easily than men, so, fellas, wait for a little guidance from her, please, and researchers find (thank heavens, or the action would die down) that women generally do about fifty percent more touching than their male counterparts. (Shall I start an international movement right about here for men to use their touches more and better? Hint, hint.) Whatever the case, women get away with touching more than men -- they can show their feelings more openly, and one of the best emotional displays is by a nice, soft, enticing touch.

An interesting point about touching is that the more you touch people in the right way, the more they respond in kind.

Imagine the tips of your fingers gliding along the smooth cheek of another person. Try to feel all the intriguing reactions within your own mind and body as you make intimate contact. Feel the response? When your hand snuggles inside the other person's hand, doesn't your heart react? Now, imagine you and your partner dancing the tango, that lovely Latin American dance that incorporates hands, arms, legs, chests or breasts, and so-on, touching to a contagious beat. Got the picture? Don't tell me those dancers are communicating as impersonally as if they were at a bridge party. No way. The messages are deep, memorable, and electrical in effect.

What are some of the intimate skin zones you should avoid touching in that first encounter? The neck, the naked shoulder (clothed is different), inside the elbow, the chest area, the buttocks, and the Taboo Zone (there's that magic territory again). These intimate spots are ultra sensitive and any touch is deciphered as sexual in intent. Touching the face connotes an intimacy you'll probably want to avoid in that first social situation .

I teach in workshops how to read the body language message in the stranger 's eyes. Sometimes you will meet someone who is nonverbally saying, "Don't come any nearer. Do not touch me." Read that message with empathy and understand that for some reason (which is no business of yours), they do not want to be touched by you. Some invalids feel this way. Abused children often want to avoid skin touching skin. Misogynists do not want you near. Whatever the reason, and they can be myriad, interpret the message and heed it carefully. Small pupils, squinted eyelids, and an eyebrow frown all say, "Do not dare touch me." I've known weird souls who think they can, from their own great attraction, break down this nonverbal rebuff immediately. Don't you waste your precious time, please.

We generally touch through handshakes, pats, hugs, caresses, kisses, brushes, squeezes, foot taps, pinches, strokes or other physical contact, and the meanings can range from a simple greeting, to showing affection and comfort, to ultimate intimate sexual contact.

If you remember only one thing from this section, let it be this: touch usually produces a more profound response than do any words. You cannot ignore touch because you are in a physical, nerve-to-nerve contact with the other person that is impossible to ignore. Think about it: the dentist's touch, the nurse's touch, the teacher's touch, as remote as they are, have an effect. (Sometimes helpful, sometimes hateful.) Take this into the personal realm, and the effect multiplies exponentially. I once had a lover who touched sometimes in very loving ways, but at other times could give aggressively: pinches, light cuffs, and an occasional buttock invasion which I believe the common people call "goose." Ha. Always accompanied with a laugh. I never could totally relate to the guy and I believe he used public sites in order for such touches to humiliate me and make him feel superior. I got rid of him.

I have had other fellows be far too intimate in initial meetings, touching too suggestively "accidentally" skimming my bosom (which isn't too hard to miss), holding the coat collar a moment too long at the neckline -- you get the picture. <u>Coming on too strong with touch</u>. They are always looking for a lady love and not finding her. Hmmm. I wonder why. When surveying females, I find they often use intimate touches daintily, but too soon in the relationship. Lots of fellows do not care for women coming on too strong, <u>too soon</u>. And touch is the revealer.

Some French wit once said that sexual intercourse is the harmony of two souls and the contact of two epiderms. Ashley Montague, author of *Touching*, says that the true language of sex is primarily nonverbal. How right he is. On this discovery voyage of yours, keep in mind that touching opens doors to finding the right mate or closes those portals resoundingly. It's all in the way you use touch.

I've seen fellows make such a miserable impression with their displays of touching etiquette that they killed what could have been the beginnings of a romance. One church I attended in California was into hugs and requested that congregants hug each other in greeting at one point in the service. We gals, after private discussions, discovered we did not want to stand near a certain fellow who was absolutely repulsive in his hugs. (Translate "hug" into offensive groping, very close breaths or gasping pants, and squeezes that just about choked the life out of the huggee.) Someone finally told him off and I guess he now attends church elsewhere, Lord have mercy on other recipients of his misguided instincts.

To repeat: sexual touches usually involve sexual areas of the body such as breasts, buttocks, pelvis, and are blatant in their sexual message. Lovers cannot resist touching the other person in some intimate way. Watch the teenage sweethearts in the malls and see how they cannot keep their hands off each other in a fashion meant for the bedroom. Watch secret lovers who are carrying on clandestine relationships and see how, in many inventive ways, they manage to brush up against each other. Touch tells the whole story.

There are taboos about touch. We Americans are slow about touching strangers, except in routine transactions such as receiving change from a cashier or accepting our purchased item. There are hurtful touches such as stepping on someone's toes or carelessly touching someone's sunburn. We always apologize when we've touched someone and our touch startled them, such as touching them from behind when they were unaware. We politely say we are sorry if our touch interrupts an activity such as touching the shoulder of a reader deeply involved in his book in a library. It's not nice to sneak up and hug someone when they are immersed in conversation with someone else. We frown on pushing someone out of the way rudely (all commuters pay attention). We don't appreciate "funny" touches that are aggressively playful -- the **toucher** is the only one having fun. ("Are we having fun yet?" "NO, you idiot!) I don't appreciate being tickled in almost any kind of situation I can think of -- it's demeaning and I don't end up laughing. I don't like Dutch rubs on my head. I don't like people shouting "Boo" around corners and then grabbing me. (This scary touch can terrorize a small child.) Got the picture? If you're the meany who pulls these stunts, stop it, smell the roses, read a book, and for pete's sake stop picking on people using the excuse that you are a wit. If you must resort to mean touches in order to feel powerful, hit a punching bag or bang a racquet ball. People are too precious..

Lastly we have the double insult touch which none of us ever forgets, so make sure you're not the toucher in this one. (If you're guilty, you deserve to be alone the rest of your life. You're beyond help.) Let's pretend you are the all-powerful boss who bawls out the employee royally, and then after the chewing out, while escorting the rebuked one to the door, chummily place your arm around the employee's shoulder. "Boy, you really blew it that time," you say, giving an ogre grin. And the shamed victim seethes in resentment and embarrassment. Here's another double insult: the husband pokes his wife gently in the stomach as she serves dessert, "Aren't you putting on a few pounds?" Or the child who is flicked on the head, "Let's don't see any more report cards like that! How does this feel, eh?" The new boyfriend touches the slip strap that is poking through the gal's neckline of her blouse and then has the effrontery to tell her! Whoops! Good bye, boyfriend. The brash Lothario at the singles' dance who approaches the new lady fair with a touch on her shoulder and the loudly enunciated words, "You're not dancing with someone?" (Of course not, why do you think she's standing here alone, Fred?) Break any of these taboos and face rejection in the form of haughty stares, indignant sniffs or outright rebuffs.

Make sure you give only positive touches to the person who may become the love of your life.

There are a couple of touches that are permissible that may let you touch the other person oh, so gently, and just a bit extra. You may refer to her necklace and then touch it ever so lightly. If you're a gal you can say, "What a handsome tie," and lightly finger the tie. The brief touch, obviously, does not inspect the apparel or appurtenance, but gives an extra fillip to the touch. There is an instrumental ancillary touch, totally unnecessary, such as handing the phone to someone and then touching their hand or wrist. It does add an additional friendly message. Handing someone good old cash or change and touching their hand deliberately in the routine exchange adds dimension. We often flirt by touching, substituting an object for our fingers, as every saucy *senorita* knows when she touches the wrist of her *caballero* with her pretty fan. The fan is a substitute for her hand and is a handy metaphor indeed, if I can get away with a bad pun.

Where does all this information help? Your usage of touch must be masterful: not too strong, not too bombastic, not too distant nor vague – just right. Check out how the other person touches. Are they overbearing? Are they kind? Are they too timid? Is their touch polite? Use your Sherlock Holmes skills to discover just who this person really is and if you want them in your life. Intimacy, remember, begins with touch.

YOU AND TOUCHING

Were you reared in an environment of easy touching with hugs and kisses freely given?

When you meet a stranger, do you offer a handshake as a matter of routine etiquette, or is touching the other person faintly repugnant to you?

When you are touched accidentally in a friendly social situation, how do you react?

If you are bumped or jostled on the sidewalk or in a mall, what is your typical reaction?

Do you ever hold hands or clasp shoulders with a friend?

If someone gives you a hug, say at church, do you find yourself patting them on the back in a friendly way, or is your back stiff and your hands immobile in a "freeze" context?

When someone is about to kiss you, do you lock your lips, compressing and tightening them in a movement of slight rebuff?

Are your elbows constantly guarding your body when you are hugged?

Are your touches often aggressive, meant to be funny but turn out to be grim instead?

Are you aware of touch etiquette and do you employ that knowledge at all times?

How do you manage the first touch when meeting someone you are interested in?

What kinds of touches turn you off and conversely, what kinds of touches turn you on?

Do you clutch a handbag or briefcase in a manner that shields your body from contact from someone's physical contact?

CHAPTER FOURTEEN - SMELL

Remember that time I saw Clark Gable knocking them unconscious at the glove counter? I must admit I was a bit intrigued not only by his masculinity, but his clean, attractive smell as well. He was faintly and distinctly marked by Brut, that lovely male-domain cologne, and any time I sniff it at some social encounter, for a second my nose almost mistakes the sweet-smelling gentleman for Mr. Gable. They say Napoleon splashed himself copiously with 4711, and Europeans connect that cologne with his charisma. That's how strong our sense of smell is—it can recall memories, personalities, encounters in enchanting or (sniff!) repugnant ways. Indeed, the nose has it.

Part of the chemistry of love is odor, often body odors. Now, in my world and probably yours, body odor is not a topic we often discuss, but it is an all-pervasive subject that guides us constantly. We react to the smell of others instantaneously. The human animal has absolutely obnoxious odors as I describe in *Body Language: First Impressions*. No one has explained this better than Desmond Morris in *The Naked Ape*. Read it if you are in doubt about our survival and its connection to stink. Our secretors of body scent are called the apocrine glands which are located in the eyelids, armpits, nipples and areolae, and the genital and anal regions. If disease-free and clean, we can pass the sniff test successfully. If we have sweated and not cleansed in any of those aforementioned regions, look out for trouble in many parts of the world – those areas that are smell-conscious.

If you want to attract a stranger, check yourself out on a sniff test before leaving home –and don't leave home without it. Make sure all parts of the body are sweet-smelling, all clothing is fresh and fragrant, and that your breath is clean and pleasantly scented. There is no substitute for clean. There is no way imaginable to effectively disguise dirty. Pigs is pigs and mud is mud and there's no getting around it. Remember the good old Boy Scout rule: "Cleanliness is next to godliness." Amen.

We Americans have the highest smell anxiety in the world. We spend millions, even billions, of hard-earned dollars in order to obliterate natural body odor using powders, creams, lotions, deodorants, douches, and perfumes. Some people consider body smells sexually attractive, but I vote that you stay clean smelling in case your potential lover really is uptight about body odor.

The scent we pick up in the first encounter is called "pheromones" and means a chemical that can be consciously detected. Pheromones are tremendously exciting to the human animal and lead to all kinds of fascinating scripts. Each of us has a unique olfactory signature, as any dog knows that can pick us out accurately at 100 paces. (Trained tracking dogs can easily do much better than that.) We are not as good as dogs at tracking, but one experiment at the University of Pennsylvania showed that both male and female human subjects could guess with 95 percent accuracy the sex of others from their breath, exhaled into a tube. Male odors were found to be more intense and unpleasant than those of females. (As if you didn't know already!) Fellas, have a heart and please do not waft locker room fragrance at us females unwarrantedly. They haven't patented a "Locker Room at 5:00 PM" cologne successfully yet.

Odorous sweat is most noticeable in the armpits where it ferments and becomes stale-smelling. Clothing that is not changed daily retains that rank smell, so fair warning – Mom said wear clean underwear for a serious reason. If I seem to be preaching atcha , it's due to terrible experiences in teaching, training, and management. (People with whom I dealt, not me.) I once had to terminate an employee for foul body odor, and talk about stinky dilemmas. The poor soul never really understood and probably still moves from job to job, needlessly offending people.

Try as we will, we cannot cover, cloak, or disguise stale, dirty odors. Soap is generally our best friend, but some people mistakenly think that perfume will work just as well. Wrong. (We'll pause for just a moment while you gasp and heave as you recall disgusting perfume combined with fermented body odor reek.) Compost pits smell better.

Do not, please, be led astray by musk perfume ads. Musk perfume only turns on a female musk ox, as it should, for musk is a strongly scented substance secreted under the skin of the abdomen of the male musk deer. People can have myriad responses to smells. Human gender chemistry has a bearing on people's sensitivity to smells. For the female, both menstruation and menopause change reactions to odor, so, gals, beware: your nose can change. And both genders, no matter the season, best have a smell check-test from a perceptive friend who will tell you the truth about your own odor.

Incidentally, remember Dr. Samuel Johnson, he of dictionary fame? He was a horribly messy, unwashed specimen and approached by a fussy aristocratic lady, he presented a pretty disgusting aura. "Dr. Johnson!" she exclaimed, "you smell.!" "No, madam," said he, bowing politely, "I stink. You smell."

What's the real message when the gentleman gives the lady flowers or perfume? "I hope this makes you chemically excited." In other words, sexually interested. When milady makes her personal odors pleasant, she is signaling to the world nonverbally (and sometimes even unconsciously) "I'm a woman. In the right set of circumstances, I'm available politely." Wouldn't florists and perfumers be shocked to know they are in the business of marketing sex.!

Each of us has our own favorite smells and it is important to remember that we bond with those who display personal body smells and surrounding environmental odors that appeal to us, that even match us. Try to hone in on the smell preference of the person you are courting, for there lies one of our strongest emotional ties. A distasteful smell can easily lose you your love; a harmonious fragrance can help us fall in love. It's all in the nose!

CHAPTER FIFTEEN - TURN ONS, AROUSALS, APHRODISIACS, AND ALL THAT STUFF

Yeah, yeah, yeah, I know. You may have kissed a hundred people and you're still looking. And kissing. But only a tiny few, perhaps just one person REALLY turns you on, arouses you sexually, makes your body chemistry work overtime to the point of surrender.

We'll talk more later about body language and sexual arousal, but first let's explore ways to increase potency. Oysters, caviar, powdered rhinoceros tusk, tiger balm, cocks' combs, monkey's paws, ground up testes of the bull elephant, avocados, figs, eggs, ambergris, ginseng, asparagus, musk, mandrake root, orchids, artichokes, black beans, crocodile semen, yohimbe, Spanish Fly, frogs' legs, meloid beetles, bull's blood (from the testes), camel's milk, cappuccino laden with rich sweet milk, garlic, onions, snails, mushrooms, rotting fish entrails, honey, vinegar, truffles, phallic-shaped fruits, and yes, even chocolate. All are considered somewhere in this world as capable of arousing sexual emotions and resultant performance. We can go on and on. Promise not to kill any animals to satisfy your lust, and beware of what you take into your body. Some of the aforementioned aphrodisiacs have proven lethal and I don't welcome litigation.

Body language points out the moment when you are sexually aroused in a series of codes fairly easy to read. Your body gives off a number of dramatic changes that announce your arousal level. For instance, for the female, the breasts signal sexual interest, particularly with the areolae swelling and the nipples becoming firm, even erect. Her uterus expands and lifts, the clitoris hardens and engorges as the vagina plumps up. For the male, the penis erects as it becomes filled with blood, the testicles swell, and his body prepares for ejaculation.

Other body parts display sexual arousal as well. Lips and skin fill with blood, nerve endings become much more sensitive, the eyes mist over and lose focus, and hearing sensitivity diminishes in order to allow you to concentrate on what's happening **inside** rather than **outside**. Muscle tone changes, sometimes causing the skin to tremble, to soften, to flush, and become moist. (Men sweat, but poets endow the female with dew.) Your facial expression may shift, perhaps getting more contorted, or you may lose facial expression completely as your body becomes overwhelmed with sensation. (Watch courting couples slow dance, oblivious to all others, and you'll see what I mean.) Your voice may soften, becoming a little deeper and husky. Your breath may change as your heart rate rises and adrenaline pumps around your body. Your smell and taste may alter, too, believe it or not, for the sebaceous glands at the edge of your lips and mouth will produce chemicals that signal your arousal, and your genitalia will change their odor as you near orgasm. The human body becomes a total sex machine, charged to climax.

All these signs make up a body language sexual code that is high-grade information and easily understood. I doubt that in the midst of arousal you examine each of these signs objectively, checking off points, but when you are in that state of arousal, you are distinctly aware that something wonderful and exciting is happening and most creatures <u>love</u> the state of arousal, wishing it to last as long as possible. You may experiment with your partner finding out what they like, what you like, and indulge each other accordingly, if my meaning is plain.

Let's take a look at the erogenous zones of each gender. Note the differences:

FEMALE EROGENOUS ZONES

Face
Behind the ears
Earlobes
Back of the neck
Breasts
Shoulders
Waist
Hands
Inside elbows
Lower stomach
Buttocks
Genitals
Thighs
Backs of knees
Feet

MALE EROGENOUS ZONES

Forehead
Earlobes
Behind the ears
Neck
Mouth
Shoulders
Inside of elbows and knees
Nipples
Hands
Small of the back
Buttocks
Genitals

A partner cannot know where you are sensitive unless you let them know, so it is important to give verbal feedback for directions to the other person. Men often become so rapt in their own pleasure that they forget to seek direction from the gal, so remember to ask for feedback.

The classic six basic universal emotions that we reviewed in facial expressions again give important data in lovemaking: a smile when happy, tears with sadness or *tristesse*, anger signs, disgust signs, surprise, and fear. Woven through these basic signs are subtler signals of other emotions: satisfaction or satiation, regret, distance, coolness, irritation, shame, embarrassment, distaste, confusion, and even anxiety, and sometimes hurt or anger are varieties of the basic six that you can read if you look hard enough. Watch out for conflicting signals, sometimes even a combination of two basic emotions can be puzzling. Try to find to an explanation that will aid the situation and ease your own tension. Not an easy task.

Sex satisfies in ways the poets never dreamed of. It wears us out, but pleasurably. It drains our juices but we cry for more and more episodes. It brings a feeling of contentment no other activity does nor any other emotion can supply. No matter our age, we seek it in some form all out lives.

CHAPTER SIXTEEN - ETIQUETTE AND LOVE

"Please" and "thank you" open more than social doors: by the way you sincerely convey consideration for the other person, and they in return, love may walk right into your heart. All those mentors who taught you courtesy knew what they were doing: they were helping you create a better you, a nicer you, and a more refined you. When we convey courtesy to the other person, nonverbally we are showing respect in a kindly fashion. Grandma was right when she said you can catch more flies with honey than vinegar, bless her wise heart.

CHIVALRY NOT-SO-TRIVIA

Back in the Middle Ages when knights chased dragons, codes of social etiquette were written and adhered to closely. How closely, you say interestedly. Very, say I, seriously. Enough so that those ancient heroes lost their heads if rules were disobeyed. Read all about Arthur and his codes of etiquette and realize these were not mythic chivalric rules. They bespoke a time and a rigid set of rules of courteous behavior.

For instance, Milady had to be protected. The umbrella covered her fair head. The knight got the slops from the upper window on his head because he walked nearest the curb, keeping her safe from overhead messes and street helter skelters. He handled the mish mash for her in a manly style.

Today's streets are a bit cleaner, but we still expect gentlemen to act like courteous, highbred, nobles. Breeding tells in your handling of etiquette, and this may be the very variable in your kit bag of tricks that wins you the prize.

Today's women can practice chivalric etiquette every bit as well as today's males. I'm adamant that if we asked for equality, then we'd better produce. Ms. Jones can help a gentleman through doors if his hands are full of packages. She can aid him in donning an overcoat. She can assume a natural, helping role whenever the occasions calls for it. The key word is "natural" – she must not act as though this is an <u>unnatural</u> burden foisted off on her by whatever rules and regs hold sway these days. Better she stay home and needlepoint dragons for the castle walls if she can't mix in today's bluster, say cold-hearted I.

Does display of etiquette help to bring you love? I hope I've convinced you that it does. Look around you in social situations and note the effects of courtesy versus rudeness in human rapport. That should convince you overwhelmingly.

Don't forget that companies often will test a prospective employee in greeting, eating, and farewell situations, so plan to incorporate all aspects of life.

Cultures show respect in different ways, but in this book I attempt to deal with middle class America in general terms. We usually do not kiss both cheeks in greeting etiquette, as do the French. Our men do not hold hands with each other as do the Arabs. We do not rub noses as do the Polynesians. Tibetans stick out their tongues, and some parts of the world pat the other guy's buttocks in greeting –hey, we consider that beyond the pale. We do not kow-tow as do the Orientals, and we do not mind showing our backsides as we depart. Generally, we do not lower the head in deferment, preferring to stand erect. We do not enter a room in order of our status except at government or military functions. We like to kick status into a cocked hat and the devil take the hindmost. *Hoi polloi* is our accepted style. We are Americans and we display etiquette as democratically as possible.

I love to remember the day dear Jimmy Carter, then President of the United States, kissed Queen Elizabeth II <u>on her cheek</u> by way of a polite Georgia farewell. They say the queen later hissed to someone, "The only man to ever do that before was my husband.!" Almost as bad as when Harry Truman took the same queen, then Princess Elizabeth, upstairs to see his eighty-year-old mother. Old Ma Truman sat up, shook the royal hand, and whispered, "I voted for your father." I guess the point of this paragraph is to accept graciously what comes naturally from other cultures and try not to be too disgruntled over differences. Politeness is important to everybody.

As I've researched people and places for this book, time and again I've been struck by rudeness displayed blatantly to the point I'd like to punch out the lights of boors in modern society. There is no excuse for overbearing rudeness, especially to strangers. (I suppose you call punching out lights rude, but say not so in a good cause!) People not offering a seat to someone physically challenged. Blatantly ignoring an older person as though age is a crime of some sort. Invading the space of children. Invasion of personal space bubbles as though all the world belongs to the bully. Acting as though a sexual persuasion different from one's own is bizarre. Downright rudeness when it comes to queuing up in stores, theatre marquees, taxi stands, exiting an airplane, etc. Lying in order to get ahead. Being late. Breaking appointments or standing up the other person without an apology. Cheating. Downright stealing. The display of courtesy in society these days has hit a downright low. It's cause for alarm.

If you are guilty of selfish behavior in order to prosper, you'd best think about your *modus operandi* again. Are you offending others in order to get your own way? Are you leaving people in your wake who secretly plan to "getcha" because of your insufferable behavior? Have you become an intolerable lout? Manners count, and when it comes to love, one needs to think about tenth century knights, troubadours, castles, chivalry, and all those good items that made romance so magical back then. The display of courtesies will smooth your way through life, so try to get an assessment of your own courteous behavior. You may not be a knight nor his lady fair, but chivalry still holds good. What grades are written on your own personal report card?

GREETING BEHAVIOR

Is the first meeting stressful for you? Are you sweaty-palmed just thinking about meeting a stranger? Each of us experiences anxiety in different ways, so practice this section of the book slowly and carefully for a superb first impression. Too much tension can ruin your body language, so try to mentally conquer all your fears before you go into a social situation which is threatening.

The manner by which we greet clues the stranger into all kinds of things about us: how carefully we were reared and trained, our own self-confidence, our willingness to meet the stranger graciously, and our respect for the status of the stranger's age, infirmity, and sex. Elegance without clumsiness is the demand here, so it is important that you practice your greeting time and again until it begins to fit properly. The superior usually takes the initiative in greeting behavior: the host, the boss, the prison warden, ...whoever. .First impressions, you know, take place in less than a minute and last for life. For a lifetime, you hear? That is the moment when we imprint on our brain at least fourteen critical variables that make or break you. Do you rise for the stranger? Do you approach him (instead of the opposite)? Is there a pleasant smile on your face, or at least a pleasant facial expression? Are your eyes friendly? Do your eyes make strong, but not too long, eye contact? Do you extend a firm handshake for the first touch? Is your hand warm, dry, firm? (Abraham Lincoln said a handshake is not a handshake if it is not employed with both hands. I follow that rule assiduously with good results, although an occasional fellow thinks I'm super-friendly.) Do you utter words of greeting? If you're mum or nil on any of these questions, grade yourself a dud at greeting. If you are not an openly giving person in the greeting scenario, plan to be interpreted as selfish, self-centered, timid, or even misanthropic.

Do you take your hostess a greeting gift, such as flowers or candy? Do you send thank-you notes subsequent to a meeting for some kindness received? Do you ever send a spontaneous, friendly note for no reason at all? Do you give a polite phone call? Do you remember birthdays with a cute card? Do you bring munchies to share with colleagues? These are all follow-ups to a friendly greeting, rounding it out to a memorable event.

When introduced to a stranger, do you say, "Pleased-ta-meetcha"? Do you say, "Hi"? Do you say "Howdy"? You'll do better if you say, "How do you do?" or "Good morning" or whatever the time of day. Art Buchwald used to say, "Dead. My mother's dead." at White House functions and get "Pleased to meet cha" in return so he knew at that point, utterances were not heeded too closely. Heed your own greetins, please.

That Buchwald story does not get you off the hook, little buddy. Stick to the script. We must go through form processes, so hang in there.

Test yourself on your attitude toward various greeting situations and see how you reveal yourself:

When talking to a stranger, I find myself backing away.
I hate walking into a room full of strangers.
I always seem to be a wallflower in social situations.
I seem to have a lot of hostilities and prejudices against a stranger. I wonder if I show it.
I fidget when I'm with strangers, can't seem to keep my hands still.
I'm judged by my physical appearance.
I can't find mutual subjects to discuss with strangers.
The party goes on and I sit in a corner, completely unnoticed.
I drink too much at parties.
I do not like to answer personal questions. It's not their business anyway!

FAREWELLS

Do not silently slip through the door and think you and your rudeness will be overlooked. Only the animal world has no formal farewell etiquette. Your lack of courtesy will be noted sometime, someplace, and you won't score a single point for cowardice or lassitude. Just like the greeting, farewell etiquette bespeaks us distinctly. We use almost the same behavior as in greeting: a handshake, sometimes a kiss or a hug, kind words, and perhaps even a wave.

I have a pet peeve about people who overstay. There should be a hook as they had in the old vaudeville stage shows that would pull the actor offstage when it was time. For pete's sake, don't linger. It may take guts, but bid your farewell and go. Just go!

Just as in greeting etiquette, the superior again takes the initiative with words and gestures. Sometimes we state we'll meet again and occasionally even nail the date and time down positively. Thanks are stated by the guest. "Good bye" and "Good night" have special time-honored status in farewells, so make sure you follow through correctly. Now, how do you rate yourself on farewell etiquette?

All in all, I've taken you through several typical scenes in everyone's life where your display of courtesy will ease your path to love, or, alas, do you in completely. If you did not shape up too well on my questions, plan to practice - practice - practice until social acts become easier for you to handle. Practice means being with people and playing your part in the farewell script. Try to observe yourself and do a post-mortem later. Rate yourself and find rough spots that need further practice. Some of my clients have sought private instruction when necessary in order to feel better about themselves in social situations. In any case, if you feel awkward, your body language will convey that message. Keep working until your body language is calm.

FAREWELL QUESTIONS

I leave a church service by the side door rather than take time to greet the minister.

I slip away at parties. No one notices my departure.

I find it awkward to say I enjoyed a party when I didn't.

I hate someone pawing me, especially when saying good-bye.

I consider loud laughter the height of rudeness when bidding a farewell.

People are too darned sensitive for their own good.

I'm not a toucher and I certainly do not make the first move regarding touches.

Why don't people like me?

I'm a good listener but not a good talker.

I have a tough time saying thank you.

I can't wait to get home after ten minutes wasted at a party.

Now, rate yourself.

Are you friendly?
Do you have social graces that need some help?
Are you missing out because you are anti-social
What skills are you now going to work to imptove?

EATING BEHAVIOR

Everything Mom told you about eating courtesies when you were a kid still applies. Elbows off the table. Chew with your mouth closed (one wonders what happened to this rule in restaurants). No eating peas off the knife. No talking with your mouth full. No smacking of the lips. No holding silverware like garden tools with clumsy fists. Cut off only one bite at a time. Butter only one-fourth of a slice of bread. Politely ask for an item, do not reach across the table. (I have one friend who routinely at the table says, "I'll have the butter." or "I'll have the catsup." I'd like to retort, "You can have it, until you say please.") Keep your silver and place setting in your allotted place at the table only and don't be a table hog. Do not treat items such as salt, pepper, sugar as yours only, and do place them back in the center of the table so everyone has access to them. Share. Do not slurp your soup. Cut off only dainty bites of food and do not cut the whole item at one fell swoop. Do not clatter your silver against the plate so it makes a distractingly rude noise. Pass items to the left around the table. It's okay to eat American style (fork in the left hand when cutting, then transferred to the right hand when actually spearing a bite to eat). Place your silver at five o'clock when finished. Fold your napkin at the meal's end and oh, yes, do keep the napkin on your lap, not the table, when eating. Please do not do what one of my kids did when I had important company over for dinner. He picked up a linen napkin and said, "What's this?" He's out of the will.

GOOD OLD PLEASE AND THANK YOU

Take a letter, Miss James. Please. Pass me the butter. Please. Get your hand off my knee. Please. Ooops! Just wanted to see if you are reading this dry old etiquette stuff. Sorry. Any request deserves a "Please." Any service rendered, be it verbal or material, rates a polite "Thank you." When anyone compliments one of my seminars or books, I at least say "Thank you. I appreciate that." The extra appreciation usually gets a smile and a warmer eye expression. It's good old Karma at work again: what you send forth will come back to you in kind. "Thank you for the beautiful flowers." "Thank you for the gorgeous diamond bracelet. Every time I wear it, I will think of you "

In Canada recently, at the Her Majesty's favorite palatial hotel, ensconced in a stuffy dining room filled with aristocratic diners, I was seated alone and thus was able to study body language in those hallowed surroundings. Each time the waiter served me, I said "Thank you," gave eye contact, and smiled. Adjoining diners never once expressed appreciation for service rendered. Came the next morning and I was on a tight time schedule. Guess who was seated and served first? I tell you courtesy pays in many ways.

My point to this chapter? Good etiquette can help bring love into your life.

CHAPTER SEVENTEEN - THE LOVER YOU SEEK

You deserve the best. After all this reading, study, probing, thinking, planning, and dreaming, your beloved must be the best! You've earned that golden lad or lassie for life.

As you seek the love of your life, try to keep in mind the qualities you want that person to embody and convey. That is a tough task because you can become enmeshed in physical attributes, image, personality, various settings, and all the distractions that divert your goals. Stay alert and keep to task.

Let's take a look at what most of us desire in the love of our life, and see if they match your desires. Research reveals that you hope your lover personifies:

HE OR SHE EMBODIES THESE CHARACTERISTICS:

Healthy
Happy
A Cockeyed Optimist
Warm
Outgoing
Caring
Generous
Self-Confident
One Who Perseveres
A Survivor
A Worker
Prudent
Fun
Softly Emotional
Strong
A Winner
Loyal
Friendly
Fair
Honest
Cheerful
A Peace Maker
Companionable
Wholesome
Capable

Fit
Healthy
Humane
Kind
Forgiving
Calm
Level-Headed
Creative
A Problem-Solver
Practical

These traits, while terrific, each and every one of them, may seem Pollyannish, but in different combinations with diverse people offer a variety of winning variables. You have to decide which are the top priority to you.

Somewhere along your journey, keep in mind also the traits you do not want to live with or marry. These are tougher to detect when you are floating in a cloud (or miasma) of love, passion, and emotion-fraught days. But try to keep in mind that these are variables that can grind you down in a long lifetime if you have to deal with them on a daily basis. Let's review the Negatives you may not want in your life; and do refer to this list regularly in order to keep on the straight and narrow:

THE UNCONGENIAL LOVER

A Gloomy Gus
Oscar-the-Grouch Personality
A Whiner
The Suffering Saint
Mean with Money
A Wimp
Timid
Selfish
Disloyal
Picky
A Judge
A Liar
A Warmonger
Lazy
A Pessimist
No Self Confidence

<u>UNCONGENIAL TRAITS</u> (CONTINUED)
Weak
Unprincipled
Vicious
Incompetent
Unhappy
Hurtful
Troublesome
Unfair
Unpopular
Unwholesome
Turbulent
Unkind
Disrespectful
Prejudiced

Do you have mental images of times when love was memorable? When I consider some of the most sentimental, romantic, memorable scenes of my life that still make me starry-eyed, I remember:

Bob, the medical doctor who waltzed me at 2:00 AM down the main street of Iowa City with feather-sized snowflakes sparkling on us in a silvery cloud. We danced in our formal attire (me with a black velvet, scarlet satin lined cloak over a white low-bodiced formal and he in his tux). I can still feel the dazzling spins, the laughter, the silence of the snow, the stars above our dizzy heads, and the kisses we exchanged as we danced into the morn.

Fred, the son of the chief justice of the Supreme Court of the state of M_____, who was a sunshine soul if there ever was one, who brought laughter and ease to everyone he met. There we were in the middle of one of the big wars (Civil, WWI, you name it – they all begin to feel the same). We left a movie theatre late at night with the street almost deserted, eerily quiet. He spied a motorcycle parked at a curb. You guessed it, "Hop on," he urged, and we spun around the block. When we got back to our starting point, there stood a cop. He just eyed us suspiciously as we parked the bike, walked away, giggling like crazy folk. And as the policeman just stood taking in our performance, Fred took a dance stance, bent me backwards down to the pavement and planted a huge kiss on me. The cop chuckled, walked away, and Fred and I strolled hand-in-hand.

The last romantic scene I recall is in jolly old England, Stratford-upon Avon, Shakespeare's hometown and a splendid night reception for a drama at the Shakespeare Theatre. Pressed in a crowd waiting for seats, and unable to move, I was inadvertently sharing fairly intimate space with a perfectly gorgeous English gentleman, tall, handsome, and charming. I swear if there is such a thing as falling in love instantaneously, that night was it. We exchanged polite banter, friendly jokes, and we both seemed curiously alone, (who could tell in that crush?), and our bodies were intensely aware of each other. Oh, but my brain liked him as well for he knew his Shakespeare, English history, and sites in the surrounding area so intriguing to the American stranger. We were "in love" for just a moment, because places were called, we were parted by people passing through and I never saw him again. But I've never forgotten those brief minutes and our heightened attraction, far beyond any sensation I've ever encountered with anyone else.

Those are the moments I wish for you. Quiet fun. Laughter mixed with heightened sensuality. A feeling as if your very skin belongs to someone else. A sensation of "I don't want to be anywhere else or with anyone else." The very moment is magic. It's as though Heaven dropped to Earth for just one brief moment in time. Love, truly, is in the air. Whoever you are, whatever you do in life, and wherever you are, you deserve magic moments of love for yourself. Those are the today's experiences that will build into tomorrow's romantic memories. Start planning romantic interludes for yourself and begin to program who your lover will be.

Remember that good old Law of Attraction? In order to attract the marvelous person who embodies all you admire, you must personify excellence yourself. (We know, you have a few weaknesses, but try to concentrate on all your positives.) Those good qualities are what you will use to attract the person you desire. If you want a happy person, you must have a cheerful appearance yourself. If you want your lover to be fair, guess what you must be. And so on, and so on. Get the message? It's all in the body language. What qualities are in your heart and head your body language reveals to the world. As you work to be The Super You, others will pick up your nonverbal message. It's amazing how the losers will just drift away from your life and the winners will enter.

You deserve the best. !

Choose the best. Love the best. May you live all your life with the best. God bless.

P.S. Send me your wedding invitation!

73

__INDEX__

BIBLIOGRAPHY

Ackerman, Diane. *A Natural History of Love.* New York: Vintage Books, 1995.

Ames, Jim. *Color Theory Made Easy.* NY: Watson-Guptil Publications, 1996.

Berne, Eric, M.D. *What Do You Say After You Say Hello? The Psychology of Human Destiny.* NY: Bantam Books, 1972.

Berscheid, Ellen and Elaine Hatfield Walston. *Interpersonal Attraction.* Reading, Mass: Addison-Wesley, 1969.

Brothers, Joyce, Ph.D. "Why We Love Who We Love," *Readers Digest* (March 1997)pp. 161-166.

Birren, Faber. *Color and Human Response.* NY:: Van Nostrand Reinhold, 1978.

_____. *The Symbolism of Color.* NY:: Carol Pub. Group, 1988.

Burns, David, M.D. *Intimate Connections.* New York: A Signet Book, NY: American Library, 1985.

Cabot, Tracy. *How To Make A Man Fall In Love With You.* NY: St. Martin's Press, 1984.

Cash, Thomas F, Ph.D. *What Do You See When You Look In The Mirror? Helping Yourself to a Positive Body Image.* NY: Bantam, 1995.

Cole-Whittaker, Terry. *Love and Power In World Without Limits.* NY: Harper Paperbacks, 1989.

Dowling, Colette. *The Cinderella Complex: Women's Hidden Fear of Independence.* NY: Pocket Books, 1981.

Dunkell, Samuel, M.D. *Sleep Positions: The Night Language of the Body.* NY: A Signet Book, New American Library, 1977.

Dyer, Wayne W., Ph.D. *You'll See It When You Believe It: The Way To Your Personal Transformation.* NY: Wm. Morrow & Co., 1989.

Fast, Barbara. *Getting Close* .NY: Berkley Books, 1979.

Fisher, Helen, Ph.D. *Anatomy of Love: A Natural History of Mating, Marriage, and Why We Stray.* NY: Fawcett Columbine, 1992.

Givens, Charles J. *Super Self: Doubling Your Personal Effectiveness.* NY: Simon & Schuster, 1993.

Givens, Dr. David B. *Love Signals.* NY: Pinnacle Books, 1983.

Glass, Lillian, Ph.D. *Attracting Terrific People.* NY: St. Martin's Press, 1997.

Hatfield, Elaine and G. William Webster. *A New Look At Love.* Reading, Mass. Addison-Wesley, 1978.

Jonas, Doris and David Jones. *Sex and Status.* NY: Stein and Day, 1975.

Key, Mary Ritchie. *Male Female Language.* Metuchen, N.J. The Scarecrow Press, 1975.

Landau, Terry. *About Faces. The Evolution of the Human Face.* NY: Anchor Books, 1989.

Miller, Ronald S. "Living Each Day As A Creative Act: An Interview with Dan Wakefield." *Science of Mind,* (April, 1997, Vol. 7, N. 4) 41-51.

Montagu, Ashley. *Touching: The Human Signiuficance of the Skin.* (2nd ed.) NY: Harper, Colophon Books, 1978.

Morganstern, Michael. *A Return to Romance: Finding It and Keeping It Alive.* NY: Ballantine Books, 1984.

Newburger, Howard M., Ph.D. and Marjorie Lee *Winners and Losers: The Art of Self-Image Modification.* NY: Signet, Signet Classics, New American Library, 1975.

Ponder, Catherine. *Open Your Mind To Receive.* Marina del Rey, CA: De Vorss & Co., 1985.

Quilliam, Susan. *Body Language: How To Understand and Master The Use of Bodytalk in the Workplace, At Home, and in Social Situations.* NY: Crescent Books, 1995.